The Tragedy of Rejecting Salvation

The Tragedy of Rejecting Salvation

by

John MacArthur, Jr.

WORD OF GRACE COMMUNICATIONS
P.O. Box 4000
Panorama City, CA 91412

All Scripture quotations, unless noted otherwise, are from the *New
Scofield Reference Bible*, King James Version. Copyright © 1967 by
Oxford University Press, Inc. Reprinted by permission.

Library of Congress Cataloging in Publication Data

MacArthur, John F.
  The tragedy of rejecting salvation.

  (John MacArthur's Bible studies)
  Includes index.
    1. Bible. N.T. Hebrews V, II–VI, 20—Criticism,
interpretation, etc.   2. Salvation—Biblical teaching.
I. Title.   II. Series: MacArthur, John F. Bible
studies.
BS2775.2.M325   1986   227'.8706   86-21726
ISBN: 0-8024-5346-5 (pbk.)

1 2 3 4 5 6 Printing/GB/Year 91 90 89 88 87 86

Printed in the United States of America

Contents

These Bible studies are taken from messages delivered by Pastor-Teacher John MacArthur, Jr., at Grace Community Church in Panorama City, California. These messages have been combined into a 4-tape album entitled *The Tragedy of Rejecting Salvation*. You may purchase this series either in an attractive vinyl cassette album or as individual cassettes. To purchase these tapes, request the album *The Tragedy of Rejecting Salvation* or ask for the tapes by their individual GC numbers. Please consult the current price list; then, send your order, making your check payable to:

WORD OF GRACE COMMUNICATIONS
P.O. Box 4000
Panorama City, CA 91412

Or call the following number:
818-982-7000

1

The Tragedy of Rejecting Full Revelation—Part 1

Outline

Introduction
A. The Content
B. The Crowd
   1. The possessors of salvation
   2. The professors of salvation
   3. The predecessors to salvation
C. The Contrast
   1. The significance of the New Covenant
   2. The superiority of the Lord Jesus Christ
D. The Counsel
   1. The first warning
   2. The second warning
   3. The third warning
E. The Changeover
   1. The appeal
   2. The approach
Lesson
I. The Warning to Non-Christians (5:10—6:8)
   A. The Problem (vv. 10-14)
      1. Dullness Prevents Understanding (vv. 10-11)
         a) Understanding the priesthood of Melchizedek
         b) Understanding the problems with dull hearing
         c) Understanding the cause of dull hearing
      2. Dullness Prevents Teaching (v. 12)
         a) The time involved
         b) The terms involved
            (1) "The first principles"
            (2) "The oracles of God"
               (a) Romans 3:1-2
               (b) Acts 7:38

    (c) 2 Samuel 16:23
  c) The tasks involved
    (1) Getting the big picture
    (2) Showing faith
    (3) Understanding the basics
  d) The truth involved
 3. Dullness Prevents Righteousness (vv. 13-14)
  a) Understanding the problem
    (1) Their lack of experience in righteousness
    (2) Their lack of discernment in spiritual matters
  b) Understanding the word *babe*
    (1) Romans 2:19-21
    (2) 1 Corinthians 3:1-2
    (3) 1 Peter 2:2
    (4) Ephesians 4:13-14
    (5) Galatians 4:3

Conclusion

Introduction

A. The Content

Hebrews 5:10—6:12 is a difficult passage of Scripture to interpret. Through the years there have been many conflicting views, even among those who call themselves evangelical.

This portion of Scripture deals with spiritual maturity. The first section (5:10—6:8) is addressed to unbelievers, and the second section (6:9-12) is addressed to believers. The theme of the epistle is the immeasurable superiority of Christianity over Judaism.

B. The Crowd

The epistle to the Hebrews was needed because a small community of Jewish people had been led to Christ by some of the apostles and prophets of the first-century church. In addition, there were some that were convinced about Christ but had neglected to make a commitment to Him for fear of reprisal from their Jewish friends.

1. The possessors of salvation

The writer of Hebrews affirms that the believers had done the right thing in responding to Christ. He encourages them not to go back to Jewish legalism with all its trappings.

2. The professors of salvation

Some people in the community were intellectually convinced and had believed the facts concerning Christ but had never made a commitment to Him. They were not unlike those in Matthew 7:21-23 of whom Jesus says, "Not every one that saith unto me, Lord, Lord, shall enter into the kingdom of heaven, but he that doeth the will of my Father, who is in heaven. Many will say to me in that day, Lord, Lord, have we not prophesied in thy name? And in thy name have cast out demons? And in thy name done many wonderful works? And then will I profess unto them, I never knew you; depart from me, ye that work iniquity." Some will stand at the judgment seat, knowing all the information about Christ and yet having failed to commit their lives to Him. To that potential group the writer of Hebrews says, "Come to salvation. Don't just stand there and neglect the most important thing of all: receiving Jesus Christ. Don't come to the edge of Christianity, only to rush out again because of your lack of commitment."

3. The predecessors to salvation

The writer also addresses Jewish people who were being exposed to the New Covenant for the first time. They had not yet heard the reality of the gospel of Christ.

C. The Contrast

Throughout the book of Hebrews, the many comparisons and contrasts are basically between Christianity and Judaism. That is the key to a proper interpretation of this epistle.

1. The significance of the New Covenant

The Holy Spirit is not contrasting two kinds of Christians—the immature versus the mature. He is contrasting the substance—Christ—with the shadow—the Old Covenant. The pattern is opposed to the reality, the visible is opposed to the invisible, and the type is opposed to the antitype. The Old Testament is a picture of what would be fulfilled in Christ in the New Testament. The central theme of the book of Hebrews is the superiority of the New Covenant to the Old, of Christianity to Judaism.

2. The superiority of the Lord Jesus Christ

One fact of the New Covenant is that it has a better

mediator—the Lord Jesus Christ. The Old Covenant in some cases was mediated by angels, and also by certain men of God, such as Moses, Aaron, Joshua, and Melchizedek. The New Covenant, however, comes through Jesus Christ and is better than that of angels and prophets. The writer of Hebrews is encouraging fellow Jews to go from Judaism to the New Covenant, which is Christianity. Judaism is the picture that points to the Messiah, Christ Himself. Since Jesus is the perfect fulfillment of all the pictures and types in the Old Covenant, the Jewish people should not cling to the shadow but to the reality behind it. The book of Hebrews, therefore, compares and contrasts the two parts of God's revelation reflected by the division in our Bibles.

D. The Counsel

Hebrews 5:10—6:12 is the third parenthetical warning given to Jews who were intellectually convinced only. Interspersed throughout the book of Hebrews are several warnings to those who were on the edge of decision but had not yet come to faith in Christ. These warnings can also be seen as encouragement and counsel to Jewish people who had trusted Christ but were tempted to turn back into Judaism because of doubts, criticism, and persecution. But it was written mainly to unbelievers.

1. The first warning

The first warning concerns neglecting the gospel of Christ. The writer says in chapter 2, "We ought to give the more earnest heed to the things which we have heard, lest at any time we should let them slip. For if the word spoken by angels was steadfast, and every transgression and disobedience received a just recompense of reward, how shall we escape, if we neglect so great salvation, which at first began to be spoken by the Lord, and was confirmed unto us by them that heard him, God also bearing them witness, both with signs and wonders, and with diverse miracles and gifts of the Holy Spirit, according to his own will" (vv. 1-4).

2. The second warning

The second warning concerns hardening one's heart to the gospel. Hebrews 3:7-12 says, "As the Holy Spirit saith, Today if ye will hear his voice, harden not your hearts, as in the provocation, in the day of trial in the wilderness, when your fathers put me to the test, proved me, and saw my works forty years. Wherefore, I was grieved with that generation, and said, They do always err in their heart, and they have not known my ways. So I swore in my wrath, They shall not enter into my rest. Take heed, brethren, lest there be in any of you an evil heart of unbelief, in departing from the living God."

3. The third warning

The third warning is in Hebrews 5:10—6:12. It concerns the issue of spiritual maturity, focusing on the danger of staying with the elemental truths and promises of the Old Covenant, even though it had been superseded by the New. It is a warning to those who have made a shallow profession of faith but are not true believers.

E. The Changeover

The third warning follows the same pattern as the first two. The only difference is that the writer is exhorting his readers to grow up to the mature truths of the New Covenant. It was time for them to no longer involve themselves with the shadow of the Old Covenant, for they were in danger of eternal judgment. The warning is not for one who is a baby Christian as opposed to a more mature Christian but for one who is still locked in Judaism as opposed to one who has come to full faith in Christ. Each warning passage in Hebrews is directed to those who are on the edge of a decision for Christ, but the passages could also be applied to a Christian who needs encouragement to continue in his knowledge of the blessings of the New Covenant.

1. The appeal

There are, of course, many exhortations in the New Testament for immature Christians to grow up. Throughout the history of the church, there has been need for such counsel, but that is not what the writer of Hebrews is primarily trying to convey. The appeal is primarily evangelistic. It is not a call for a Christian to grow in the faith but for an unbeliever to come into the faith—into the mature truths and blessings of the New Covenant. This is the same maturity or perfection described in Hebrews 10:1, 14, which uses the Greek word *teleioō* in the context of salvation, not Christian growth.

2. The approach

Judaism is the ABC's of Christianity. The Old Covenant is

the spiritual alphabet on which the New Covenant is built. You do not use an encyclopedia to start teaching children to read. You use pictures and visual objects to explain what needs to be learned. Later you will begin to teach them truths from the foundational pictures you've built on. The Old Testament is God's elementary, foundational teaching. He has since moved on to the reality, which is Christ Himself (Col. 2:16-17, NASB*). All the feasts, sacrifices, and ceremonies pictured in the Old Testament pointed to the reality of Christ. The issue the writer of Hebrews was dealing with was that many of his readers had professed a belief in Christ but were still clinging to the elemental patterns of Judaism. They were in great danger of reaching a point beyond salvation. The writer is pleading for them to leave the pictures, the milk, and the baby food of the Old Testament, and come to the fulfilled realities and solid food of the New Testament. He wanted them to leave Judaism and come to Christ.

Lesson

I. THE WARNING TO NON-CHRISTIANS (5:10—6:8)

"[Christ is] called of God an high priest after the order of Melchizedek. Of whom we have many things to say, and hard to be uttered, seeing ye are dull of hearing. For when for the time ye ought to be teachers, ye have need that one teach you again the first principles of the oracles of God, and are become such as have need of milk, and not of solid food. For everyone that useth milk is unskillful in the word of righteousness; for he is a babe. But solid food belongeth to them that are of full age, even those who by reason of use have their senses exercised to discern both good and evil. Therefore, leaving the principles of the doctrine of Christ, let us go on unto perfection, not laying again the foundation of repentance from dead works, and of faith toward God, of the doctrine of baptisms, and of laying on of hands, and of resurrection of the dead, and of eternal judgment. And this we will do, if God permit. For it is impossible for those who were once enlightened, and have tasted of the heavenly gift, and were made partakers of the Holy Spirit, And have tasted the good word of God, and the powers of the age to come, if they shall fall away, to renew them again unto repentance, seeing they crucify to themselves the Son of God afresh, and put him to an open

New American Standard Bible.

12

shame. For the earth, which drinketh in the rain that cometh often upon it, and bringeth forth herbs fit for them by whom it is tilled, receiveth blessing from God; but that which beareth thorns and briers is rejected, and is near unto cursing, whose end is to be burned."

A. The Problem (vv. 10-14)

   1. Dullness Prevents Understanding (vv. 10-11)

   Before the readers of Hebrews could fully understand the significance of Jesus' priesthood being like Melchizedek's, they needed to get beyond their limited, immature understanding of God. The Holy Spirit's desire in the heart of this epistle is to emphasize the priesthood of Jesus Christ. His reasoning is clear: Because of the centrality of the priesthood in the Judaistic system, it is important for the Jewish people to know that the great high priest in the New Covenant is Christ Himself (Heb. 4:14). To prove that Christianity is greater than Judaism, the writer shows that Jesus is a greater priest than Aaron, who was the greatest high priest in the Levitical system. Not only is Jesus greater than Aaron, but He is also of an entirely different order: the order of Melchizedek.

   a) Understanding the priesthood of Melchizedek

   Verse 10 says that Christ is "called of God an high priest after the order of Melchizedek." Melchizedek first appears in Genesis 14. The only other information about him appears in Psalm 110 and Hebrews 5-7. The writer of Hebrews endeavors to explain the relationship between Jesus and Melchizedek but is unable to because his readers were "dull of hearing" (v. 11). Their dullness of hearing was spiritual lethargy. The relation of Melchizedek and the priesthood to Christ is rich, meaningful, and important to the flow of the book, but it cannot be understood by unbelievers, even ones who intelligently accept the gospel (1 Cor. 2:14-15).

   b) Understanding the problems with dull hearing

   The Greek word for "dull" is *nōthros*, which is made up of the Greek words for "no" and "push." When used of a person it generally refers to someone who is intellectually numb or thick. In this context it refers to spiritual dullness in terms of apprehending the truth.

When a person is spiritually dull, he is difficult to teach. You must be keen, alert, and awake in order to apprehend rich, deep truth. Because of their lack of commitment, those who were only intellectually convinced had been lulled to sleep by neglect, and that had hardened their hearts. The more someone hears the gospel without making a commitment to Christ, the more hardened and sluggish he will become.

Although this passage is not addressed to believers, the same principle applies: When we do not trust or act on any part of God's truth that we know, we become hardened to it and less likely to benefit from it. That can happen to a preacher or a teacher who does not bother to teach the deeper and sometimes harder truths of Scripture—or is afraid to do so. Paul was able to say that he did not fail to declare the whole counsel, or will, of God (Acts 20:27). No faithful servant of God will accommodate his teaching for the dull, lazy Christian.

c) Understanding the cause of dull hearing

The implication of verse 11 is that those who were dull of hearing were not always like that. They had been alert, interested, and perhaps even eager to learn more of the gospel. They did not start that way; their dullness was a gradual process. They were no doubt part of the group mentioned in 6:4 as having "once been enlightened" and had "tasted of the heavenly gift." They had come to the edge of salvation, but they began to neglect the gospel (2:1-4), hardening their hearts (3:15-19), and, tragically, were in danger of falling away (6:6-11). The Holy Spirit had been leading them step-by-step to faith in Jesus Christ, but they began to neglect His work in their lives (6:4). With their Judaistic friends pulling on them, they arrived at a settled state of spiritual stupidity.

2. Dullness Prevents Teaching (v. 12)

The writer says in verses 12, "For when for the time ye ought to be teachers, ye have need that one teach you again the first principles of the oracles of God, and are become such as have need of milk, and not of solid food."

a) The time involved

The phrase "for the time" gives us the backdrop for understanding these verses. Because of the length of

14

time they had received instruction on New Testament truth, the Hebrews should have known enough to be teaching it themselves. Not only were they not teaching it, but they also had never truly accepted it, or committed themselves to its transforming power. They had the truth in a factual and superficial way, but the truth did not have them.

There are many professing Christians—even well-known theologians—who know Scripture and the biblical languages well but do not accept or apply it. Because of the time they have spent studying the Word of God, they ought to be excellent teachers, but instead they do not even comprehend the fundamentals. They may attempt to teach the Word of Christ, but they do not even know the Christ behind the Word.

The apostles had labored long and hard among those who were intellectually convinced but not saved. The truth was in their grasp, as Hebrews 6:4 suggests: "Those who were once enlightened, and have tasted of the heavenly gift, and were made partakers of the Holy Spirit, and have tasted the good word of God, and the powers of the age to come." They had received full revelation from God, yet ultimately chose against Him.

A Spiritually Sluggish Young Girl

Some time ago I spoke at a Christian youth conference on the subject of choosing the right mate. After one of the sessions a young girl came to me and asked if we could talk about her relationship with her boyfriend. As we sat on the chapel steps, she began telling me that her boyfriend tried to convince her that whatever someone does—be it premarital sex or anything else—is all right as long as no one gets hurt. After some questioning, I found out that her boyfriend was twenty-one. She was only fourteen. When I reminded her of what God says about sex outside of marriage, she hung her head and said, "I know that. I need to be saved." She also revealed that she had not only been raised in the church but also that her dad was a pastor. I replied, "Then you know how to be saved." "No," she responded, "I've heard my father preach on it, but I don't understand it." She was a picture of spiritual sluggishness, for she had heard the gospel all her life, but she had rejected Jesus Christ for so long that her senses were dulled by sin. The gospel became so unclear to her that she could no longer understand it. She thought her father's sermons were boring and made no sense. It was not that there was something wrong with the message; it was that she was indifferent to the Word of God. I carefully delineated the gospel to her, and then we prayed together and she confessed Christ as her Lord and Savior.

b) The terms involved

(1) "The first principles"

Because they had become spiritually listless, those who were informed but unbelieving needed to be taught again the basics of Scripture (v. 12). The Greek word for "principles" is *stoicheia*, which means "elementary principles" or "that which comes first." It is used to speak of the elementary letters of an alphabet, the basic elements of the earth, the basics of geometric proof, or the elementary principles in philosophy. Since verse 12 says "first principles," it is referring to the first in a series or the very beginning of something.

(2) "The oracles of God"

The writer of Hebrews is exhorting these unbelieving Jewish people of their need to be taught the basics. The phrase "oracles of God" in verse 12 does not refer to the gospel. Because this was a Jewish audience, the oracles of God to them would be God's laws as revealed by Him in the Old Testament. And having been entrusted with the oracles of God was a great advantage to the Jewish people.

(a) Romans 3:1-2—Paul said, "What advantage, then, hath the Jew? . . . Much every way, chiefly because unto them were committed the oracles of God." This is a direct reference to the Jewish heritage of receiving the Old Testament law.

(b) Acts 7:38—Stephen said of Moses, "This is he that was . . . in the wilderness with the angel who spoke to him [Moses] in Mount

Sinai, and with our fathers, who received the living oracles to give unto us."

(c) 2 Samuel 16:23—Scripture says this about David's former adviser: "The counsel of Ahithophel, which he counseled in those days, was as if a man had inquired at the oracle of God."

It was the basic principles of Old Testament law that the Jewish readers needed to remember. They were getting considerable exposure to the New Covenant but had apparently forgotten the Old. They needed a teacher to instruct them again about the meaning of their own law. They needed to move from the picture and bring Christ into focus. The elementary principles or picture-truths were the ordinances, ceremonies, sacrifices, holy days, and washings—all foreshadowing the person of Christ. The Hebrews could not recognize Him unless they understood the pictures.

c) The tasks involved

(1) Getting the big picture

The New Testament goes beyond the ABC's of the Old Testament. The writer is calling for his Jewish audience to gain a more mature knowledge based on God's revealed Word. This is Paul's argument in Galatians 3:23-25: "Before faith came, we were kept under the law, shut up unto the faith which should afterwards be revealed. Wherefore, the law was our schoolmaster to bring us unto Christ, that we might be justified by faith. But after faith is come, we are no longer under a schoolmaster." "Schoolmaster" refers to the law's function as a tutor to lead us to Christ. Under the New Covenant, we're not under the schoolmaster (law) anymore. Since Christ has arrived, the shadow is replaced with the substance; the picturebook is replaced with writings we can read.

(2) Showing faith

All that the Hebrews knew of the truths of God should have led to a response of faith, but instead they were holding to old Judaistic patterns and would not let go. They had been taught to the point of being able to be teachers themselves, but because of their rejection and continual hard-heartedness, they had become spiritually slug-gish and needed to be reminded of the basic elements of their own Scriptures. They had to relearn the alphabet! How could the writer of Hebrews speak of Christ as the High Priest after the order of Melchizedek when they couldn't begin to understand what that meant (vv. 10-11)?

(3) Understanding the basics

Paul says in Romans 2:17-21: "If thou art called a Jew, and resteth in the law, and makest thy boast of God, and knowest his will, and approvest the things that are more excellent, being instructed out of the law, and art confident that thou thyself art a guide of the blind, a light of them who are in darkness, an instructor of the foolish, a teacher of babes, who hast the form of knowledge and of the truth in the law—thou, therefore, who teach-est another, teachest thou not thyself?" The Jew-ish people had prided themselves that they were great teachers, but in Hebrews 5:12 the Holy Spirit says they themselves needed to go back to kindergarten.

d) The truth involved

The writer of Hebrews ends verse 12 by saying they had "become such as have need of milk, and not of solid food." It is characteristic of a baby that he can handle only milk. He does not come to need milk; he is born with that need. The only person who comes to need milk—to need baby food—is one who has reverted back to childhood. Instead of becoming more mature, these people were slipping back into spiritual infancy. If you aren't progressing, then you are regressing. It is so easy for people to hear the gospel time and time again until it becomes common-place, and they gradually turn their backs to Christ.

3. Dullness Prevents Righteousness (vv. 13-14)

a) Understanding the problem

(1) Their lack of experience in righteousness

The writer of Hebrews says in verse 13, "Everyone that useth milk is unskillful in the word of righteousness; for he is a babe." The word for "unskillful" is the Greek word *apeirōs*, which means "without experience." The *a* at the beginning of the word is called an alpha privitive and is used to negate the meaning of the word following it. These Jewish readers were without experience in righteousness and were therefore unprepared to receive true knowledge of God. Those who fail to go beyond the elemental things (milk) have not really experienced true righteousness.

A spiritual babe is not accustomed to deeper truths. He cannot digest them any more than an infant can digest a steak. One who constantly lives on nothing but the Old Testament is going to find himself lacking in righteousness. A spiritual child could get some meaning out of the pictures and types of the Old Testament but not the full picture unless he also studied the word of righteousness, which is in the New Testament. Verse 13 cannot refer to a Christian because a Christian has been made righteous in Christ (2 Cor. 5:21). The term *babe* never refers to a new Christian in the New Testament, only to those who are immature.

(2) Their lack of discernment in spiritual matters

The writer of Hebrews goes on to say, "Solid food belongeth to them that are of full age, even those who by reason of use have their senses exercised to discern both good and evil" (v. 14). The contrast here is simple: A baby will stick almost anything into its mouth, for it is unable to discern what is good or bad. Likewise, one who continues to feed only on God's elementary revelations is not going to grow or have adequate discernment. The mature adult, on the other hand, has developed considerable discernment about what is right and wrong, true and false, helpful and harmful, righteous and unrighteous.

The unsaved Hebrews were sluggish and dull of hearing, unable to discern that true righteousness comes only through Jesus Christ. Jesus told the Jewish leaders of His day to "search the Scriptures; for in them ye think ye have eternal life; and they are they which testify of me" (John 5:39). The readers of the book of Hebrews needed to go past the elementary principles of the Old Covenant and develop an understanding of Christ and the New Covenant. Maturity comes through exercise, alertness, and awareness.

b) Understanding the word *babe*

The writer uses the word *babe* in verse 13 to refer only to one who is without spiritual knowledge. The term does not necessarily imply salvation. Many have used the term "babe in Christ" to refer to someone who is a new Christian. It may be true that one who is new in Christ is a babe, but the Scriptures never use the term in that context. It basically refers to immature believers, but can refer to non-believers.

(1) Romans 2:19-21—Paul chastised the Jewish teachers of his day, saying, "Art [thou] confident that thou thyself art . . . an instructor of the foolish, a teacher of babes, who hast the form of knowledge and of the truth in the law—thou, therefore, who teachest another, teachest thou not thyself?" In Jewish culture, a babe was anyone who was uninstructed. This passage is simply describing an individual who was ignorant in his knowledge of God. The term *babe* could be used as an analogy for someone who is a new Christian, but the writers of Scripture didn't choose to use it as such. It is used to talk about immature Christians, not new ones.

(2) 1 Corinthians 3:1-2—Paul said to the Corinthians, "I brethren, could not speak unto you as unto spiritual, but as unto carnal, even as unto babes in Christ. I have fed you with milk, and not with solid food; for to this time ye were not able to bear it, neither yet now are ye able." For one-and-one-half years, the apostle Paul had taught the Corinthians. Now he was writing them as much as five years later, so they were believers for approximately six years at the time. Paul's assessment of

these believers was not that they were new Christians but carnal ones. The Corinthian problem was not their infancy but their disobedience, which included divisions, envying, and strife. He could not feed them with solid food—they required milk. The difference between the Corinthians and those to whom the writer of Hebrews spoke was that the Corinthians were "babes *in Christ*" (emphasis added).

(3) 1 Peter 2:2—Peter was speaking of believers when he said, "As newborn babes, desire the pure milk of the word, that ye may grow by it." That is not a contradiction to Paul's statement in 1 Corinthians 3:1. He is simply using the same metaphor in a different way. This reference is simply describing what every dependent child needs: nourishment. While Paul says to move on from the milk, Peter says to desire the pure milk of the word. Paul uses the metaphor of a baby and milk in one way, and Peter uses it in another. Peter uses the Greek word *brephos*, which refers to a newborn, while Paul uses the Greek word *nēpios*, which refers to someone who is childish, unskilled, or simple.

The writer of Hebrews uses *nēpios* in verse 13 to refer to someone who is spiritually ignorant of the New Covenant. He was encouraging his Jewish audience to leave Judaism and arrive at the truth of Christianity.

(4) Ephesians 4:13-14—Paul said, "Till we all come in the unity of the faith, and of the knowledge of the son of God, unto a perfect man, unto the measure of the stature of the fullness of Christ; that we henceforth be no more children, tossed to and fro, and carried about with every wind of doctrine." Here, Paul uses the Greek word *teknon*, which refers to an infant or a small child. It refers to Christians in this passage, but a completely different word is used in Hebrews 5:13.

(5) Galatians 4:3—Paul also said, "We, when we were children, were in bondage under the elements of the world." This clearly refers to our former unregenerate state. Before you were

saved, you were a babe and were under the
slavery of the world's evil system.

The New Testament uses three different words for the term *babe*.
We cannot say that since it is used sometimes to refer to
Christians, it therefore refers to Christians at all points (cf. Gal.
4:3). Hebrews 5:13 refers to unsaved Jewish people who were
enlightened about Christ but had not yet received Him. The
writer goes on to warn them in 6:4-6 that they are in danger of
being eternally lost.

Conclusion

Because the writer of Hebrews goes on to explain the significance
of Melchizedek in chapter 7, he obviously expects his readers to
mature spiritually before they read this part of his message. Dr.
Charles Feinberg, one of my old seminary professors, used to say
that Judaism is the infancy the Jewish person must leave to go on
to the maturity of faith in the New Covenant Messiah. Don't
come to the edge of salvation and harden your heart toward Jesus
Christ. Come to Christ while there is still time and the excitement
is still there. And the message for the Christian is this: If it's
intolerable for someone who is convinced of the truth to be
ignorant, how much more intolerable is it for someone who not
only knows the truth but also trusts in the Son of God to be
spiritually immature!

Focusing on the Facts

1. Who is being addressed in Hebrews 5:10—6:12 (see p. 8)?
2. What is the theme of the epistle to the Hebrews (see p. 8)?
3. List three types of people with which the writer of Hebrews is
   concerned (see pp. 8-9).
4. Throughout the book of Hebrews, the many comparisons and
   contrasts are basically between _____ and _____ (see
   p. 9).
5. True or False: The Holy Spirit is contrasting two kinds of
   Christians in the book of Hebrews: mature Christians versus
   immature ones who are struggling with their faith (see p. 9).
6. Who is the mediator of the New Covenant? Who was the Old
   Covenant mediated by (see p. 10)?
7. Describe the warnings given in the book of Hebrews. Is there any
   difference between the warnings? Explain your answer (see pp.
   10-11).
8. What is meant by the term "Old Covenant" (see pp. 11-12)?

9. The Holy Spirit's desire in the heart of this epistle is to emphasize the _____ of Jesus Christ (see p. 13).
10. True or false: The more someone hears the gospel without making a commitment to Christ, the more hardened he will become toward it (see p. 14).
11. Although Hebrews 5:10—6:8 is not addressed to believers, does it have any application for believers? Explain (see p. 14).
12. What should have been the response of the Jewish people who had been under the instruction of New Testament truth (Hebrews 5:12; see p. 15)?
13. Explain what is meant by the phrase "the oracles of God" (see p. 16).
14. Is verse 13 referring to a Christian? Explain your answer (see p. 19).
15. True or false: You can be a Christian without being made righteous positionally in Christ (see p. 19).
16. How does the writer of Hebrews use the word *babe* in verse 13 (see p. 20)?
17. How does Scripture use the word *babe*? Explain your answer from the passages given (see pp. 20-22).
18. What does the author of Hebrews warn his Jewish readers about in 6:4-6 (see p. 22)?
19. What is the message for Christians in Hebrews 5:10-14 (see p. 22)?

Pondering the Principles

1. Hebrews 5:10—6:12 is a warning to those who had made a shallow profession of faith in Christ but were unwilling to submit their lives to Him. Believing in Christ involves more than just an acknowledgement of various facts about him; it is committing your life in obedience to Him because of who He is and what He did. John 8:31-32 says, "Then said Jesus to those Jews who believed on him, If ye continue in my word, then are ye my disciples indeed; and ye shall know the truth, and the truth shall make you free." Look up the following verses, which define how a person is saved, and ask God to let you know for sure whether you are really saved: Ephesians 2:8-10, Titus 3:5, and 2 Thessalonians 1:7-9.

2. First John 3:10 says, "By this the children of God and the children of the devil are obvious: anyone who does not practice righteousness is not of God" (NASB). As a Christian, your life ought to be marked by righteous behavior. Does righteousness characterize your life? Do you desire to live in daily obedience to God? If not,

you are, as were the first readers of Hebrews, in danger of self-deception. Verbally inviting Christ into your life does not make you a Christian; committing your entire life in obedience to Jesus Christ as your Lord and Savior does. Read Titus 1:16 and Hebrews 12:14 and ask Jesus Christ to give you a new heart and make you the kind of person He wants you to be.

2
The Tragedy of Rejecting Full Revelation—Part 2

Outline

Introduction

Review
I. The Warning to Non-Christians (5:10—6:8)
   A. The Problem (5:10-14)
      1. Dullness Prevents Understanding (vv. 10-11)
         a) Understanding the priesthood of Melchizedek
         b) Understanding the problems with dull hearing
         c) Understanding the cause of dull hearing
      2. Dullness Prevents Teaching (v. 12)
         a) The time involved
         b) The terms involved

Lesson
   B. The Solution (6:1-8)
      1. The need for maturity (v. 1a)
         a) Separation
         b) Salvation
      2. The need for a new foundation (vv. 1b-2)
         a) "Repentance from dead works"
            (1) Acts 20:21
            (2) Acts 26:19-20
         b) "Faith toward God"
            (1) Acts 2:38
            (2) Acts 11:17-18
         c) "The doctrine of baptisms"
            (1) Ezekiel 36:25-26
            (2) Titus 3:5
            (3) John 3:5
         d) "Laying on of hands"
         e) "Resurrection of the dead"

        (1) In the Old Testament
           (a) Job 19:25-27
           (b) Daniel 12:2
        (2) In the New Testament
           (a) John 11:25
           (b) 1 Corinthians 15
           (c) 1 John 3:2
    f) "Eternal judgment"
        (1) In the Old Testament
        (2) In the New Testament
           (a) Romans 8:1
           (b) 1 Corinthians 3:12-15
           (c) Matthew 25:46
           (d) Revelation 20:11-12
           (e) John 5:22
3. The need for power (v. 3)
    a) The writer's perspective
    b) The Lord's perspective
4. The need for remembrance (vv. 4-5)
    a) They had been enlightened
        (1) Matthew 4:16
        (2) John 1:9
        (3) 2 Peter 2:20
    b) They had tasted the heavenly gift
        (1) John 4:10
        (2) John 6:32, 53
    c) They were partakers of the Holy Spirit
    d) They had tasted the good word of God
    e) They had tasted the powers of the age to come
5. The need for a response (v. 6)
    a) The apostasy
    b) The attitude
    c) The action
6. The need for an illustration (vv. 7-8)

Introduction

Hebrews 5:10—6:12 discusses the issue of spiritual maturity. It contains the third parenthetical warning in the book of Hebrews to Jewish people who were intellectually convinced of the gospel but who had never made a real commitment to Jesus Christ.

These Hebrews knew the truth, believed it, and were even following some patterns consistent with Christianity. But they were not true Christians. They are warned periodically throughout the book of Hebrews that simply believing things about Christ without a commitment to Him is not sufficient for salvation (cf. James 2:19). They were warned after having heard the gospel and becoming so familiar with it without receiving it that they would find themselves falling away into hardhearted unbelief. It would then be impossible for them to be saved.

The contrast in Hebrews 5:10—6:12 is not between a mature Christian and an immature one but between a true Christian and a false one. The term *babe* in Hebrews 5:13 describes an unbeliever—a Jewish person who was hanging on to the ABC's of the Old Covenant. The mature person talked about in verse 14 is one who grows up by putting his faith in Jesus Christ and accepting the fuller revelation in the New Testament.

Those who were still hanging on to the Old Covenant were warned that if they continued to neglect true salvation, they were in danger of being lost forever. This passage has special significance to anyone who comes to the edge of salvation. People can go to church for years and hear the gospel over and over again, yet never really make a commitment to obey Jesus Christ.

Review

I. THE WARNING TO NON-CHRISTIANS (5:10—6:8)

    A. The Problem (5:10-14; see pp. 13–22)

        1. Dullness Prevents Understanding (vv. 10-11; see pp. 13-14)

            a) Understanding the priesthood of Melchizedek (see p. 13)

            The problem the writer of Hebrews dealt with in verses 10-11 was his readers' lack of understanding concerning the priesthood of Melchizedek. He says, "Of whom [Melchizedek] we have many things to say, and hard to be uttered, seeing ye are dull of hearing" (v. 11).

            b) Understanding the problems with dull hearing (see pp. 13-14)

            The phrase "dull of hearing" means "slow," "sluggish," or "stupid." The writer was saying that his audience was spiritually immature and, therefore, could not comprehend the deeper truths concerning the Melchizedekian priesthood. They had become neglectful of the truth they had received (2:1), hardened their hearts (3:15), and now had become sluggish in their thinking. They were now in danger of being eternally lost because of their unbelief (6:6).

  c) Understanding the cause of dull hearing (see p. 14)

 2. Dullness Prevents Teaching (v. 12; see pp. 14-18)

  a) The time involved (see pp. 14-16)

Considering the length of time and the amount of information they had had, the Hebrews could have been teachers of New Covenant truths and yet they themselves needed to be taught. They were still acquainting themselves with the elemental principles of the Old Testament. Like slow seminary students, they needed a good remedial course in Old Testament.

  b) The terms involved (see pp. 16-17)

The author says they needed to be taught again "the first principles of the oracles of God" (v. 12). He was referring to the law and promises of the Old Testament. They were in such a state of spiritual lethargy that the writer had to go back and teach them the Old Covenant before he could teach them about the New.

Lesson

B. The Solution (6:1-8)

 1. The need for maturity (v. 1*a*)

"Therefore, leaving the principles of the doctrine of Christ, let us go on unto perfection."

Understanding the word *leaving* and the phrase "go on unto perfection" is the crux in interpreting Hebrews 6:1-8. They describe the first steps the Hebrews were to make to become spiritually mature. They needed to sever once and for all their ties with the Old Covenant—Judaism—and accept Jesus Christ as Savior. They needed to do it immediately, without further hesitation. If the writer were talking only to Christians who needed to mature spiritually, he wouldn't have been able to demand instant spirituality because there is no such thing. He was speaking to Jewish people who needed to gain the maturity that salvation brings with the reception of the New Covenant. He was not talking about the process of sanctification but the instantaneous miracle of salvation. The maturity talked about here would happen when they left the ABC's of the Old Covenant to come to the full revelation in the New Testament.

a) Separation

The Greek word for "leaving" is *aphiēmi*, which means "to forsake," "put away," "disregard," or "put off." It refers to a total detachment from a previous location or position. It does not mean to build on or add something. It refers to cutting something off or moving away from something. The preposition at the beginning of the word, *aph* implies separation. The basic idea means separation from an original condition. *The Expositor's Greek Testament* translates Hebrews 6:1, "Let us abandon [give up] the elementary teaching about Christ" (W. Robertson Nicoll, ed., vol. 4 [Grand Rapids: Eerdmans, 1974 reprint], p. 293). Henry Alford comments, "Therefore . . . leaving (as behind, and done with; in order to go on to another thing)" (*The Greek Testament*, vol. 4 [Chicago: Moody, 1958], p. 104).

(1) Matthew 13:36—Matthew said, "Then Jesus sent the multitude away, and went into the house; and his disciples came unto him, saying, Explain unto us the parable of the tares of the field." The point to see in the passage is that the same preposition is used as Jesus sent them away from one place to another.

(2) Mark 4:36—Mark said, "When they had sent away the multitude, they took him even as he was in the boat." The same Greek construction is indicated with preposition. He doesn't say to build up something but to leave here and go somewhere else.

(3) 1 Corinthians 7:11—Paul said, "But and if she depart, let her remain unmarried, or be reconciled to her husband; and let not the husband put away his wife." The phrase "put away" is the same word in Hebrews 6:1, *aphiēmi*, which in this

context refers to divorce. This passage can have no other meaning than separation. It is wrong to leave a marriage, but it is mandatory to leave Judaism for Christ. The unbelieving Jewish person must separate himself from his old traditions before he can be saved.

(4) Matthew 9:2—Jesus said, "Son, be of good cheer; thy sins be forgiven [*aphiēmi*] thee." He essentially was saying "Thy sins be separated from thee." *Aphiēmi* is often used in this sense (cf. Rom. 4:7; James 5:15).

(5) Matthew 15:14—Jesus said, "Let them alone; they are blind leaders of the blind." *Aphiēmi* is used here to speak of separating oneself from false teachers.

(6) Mark 1:20—Mark said, "Straightway he called them; and they left their father, Zebedee in the boat with the hired servants, and went after him." *Aphiēmi* here refers to James and John's leaving their father to follow Jesus. As far as their life's work was concerned, they abandoned—completely separated themselves from—their father and his fishing business.

The writer is saying that the Hebrews needed to abandon their Old Testament rituals—not merely add Jesus to them. We know Hebrews 6:1 must refer to an unbeliever because at no time does the Word of God ever command Christians to drop the basics of Christianity and go on to something else. In fact, we're clearly told not to do that (cf. Gal. 1:6-9, 1 Tim. 4:1). It specifically refers to unbelievers who needed to drop the Old Covenant and move on to Christ. Our author is commanding the Hebrews to go beyond the shadows, types, pictures, and sacrifices of the Old Testament and come to the reality of Jesus Christ in the New Covenant.

Hebrews 6:1 can be translated this way: "Therefore, finally moving on from the basic principles behind the teaching of the Messiah, let's go on to maturity." The Greek translation is literally, "Leaving the beginning teaching of Messiah." They were to leave the pictures and types in the Old Testament that pointed to the coming of Messiah because He had already come!

b) Salvation

The writer of Hebrews urges his readers to "go on to perfection." The meaning of the word *perfection* is "maturity." The only way this maturity would come about is through a relationship with Jesus Christ. Hebrews 7:11 says, "If, therefore, perfection were by the Levitical priesthood . . . what further need was there that another priest should rise after the order of Melchizedek?" The writer is saying that if you could be mature by the Old Covenant, you wouldn't need Christ. The term *perfection* thus refers to the need to mature from the basics of the Old Covenant to the richness and fullness of the New.

The writer is not asking his Christian readers to grow up. He is asking his Jewish readers to drop the Old Covenant and accept the New. The same idea is seen in Hebrews 7:19: "The law made nothing perfect, but the bringing in of a better hope did." That better hope is none other than our Lord Jesus Christ Himself, who is perfection incarnate. Hebrews 10:14 says, "By one offering he hath perfected forever them that are sanctified." The writer is telling his Jewish audience to go on to perfection—to the full maturity of a relationship with the Messiah.

2. The need for a new foundation (vv. 1b-2)

"Not laying again the foundation of repentance from dead works, and of faith toward God, of the doctrine of baptisms, and of laying on of hands, and of resurrection of the dead, and of eternal judgment."

The foundation concerning the Messiah was originally laid with pictures and types, but now, the writer says, the reality is here. He gives six features of the Old Testament covenantal foundation. Many people have assigned these passages to Christians, saying they should rid themselves of the basics of the Christian life and grow up to more mature doctrines. But it could not mean that because he was specifically speaking to Jewish people who would be the only ones who could best understand those Old Testament concepts.

31

a) "Repentance from dead works"

This phrase simply refers to turning away from evil deeds. The writer says in Hebrews 9:13, "If the blood of bulls and of goats, and the ashes of an heifer sprinkling the unclean, sanctifieth to the purifying of the flesh, how much more shall the blood of Christ, who through the eternal Spirit offered himself without spot to God, purge your conscience from dead works to serve the living God?"

The Old Testament taught that a man should repent and turn from his evil works, for they bring about death. Ezekiel 18:4 says, "The soul that sinneth, it shall die." The New Testament contains a similar concept: "The wages of sin is death" (Rom. 6:23). The Old Testament contained only the first half of repentance—toward God. All men knew was to turn away from their evil works and turn toward God. But in the New Testament, repentance toward God is linked with faith in Jesus Christ. When John the Baptist came preaching, and even in Jesus' own early ministry, the message was, "Repent for the kingdom is at hand" (Matt. 3:2; 4:17). Only repentance was preached. The doctrine became more mature and complete in Jesus Christ.

(1) Acts 20:21—Paul said, "Testifying both to the Jews, and also to the Greeks, repentance toward God, and faith toward our Lord Jesus Christ." You must not only repent but also place your faith in Jesus Christ. That is why Jesus says in John 14:6, "No man cometh unto the Father, but by me." Acts 4:12 reiterates the same message: "Neither is there salvation in any other; for there is no other name under heaven given among men, whereby we must be saved."

(2) Acts 26:19-20—Paul said, "O King Agrippa, I was not disobedient unto the heavenly vision, but showed first unto them at Damascus, and at Jerusalem, and throughout all the borders of Judaea, and then to the Gentiles, that they should repent and turn to God, and do works fit for repentance." Later in verse 23 Paul says, "That Christ should suffer . . . and should rise from the dead, and should show light unto the

people, and to the Gentiles." In the New Covenant, whenever men were commanded to repent and turn toward God, it was with a view toward faith in Jesus Christ. The doctrine of repentance from dead works is made full by the doctrine of repentance toward God through faith in Christ. A person, no matter how sincerely he seeks, who does not repent of his sins and turn to faith in Jesus Christ, will never reach God. Jesus Christ is the only way God has provided to Himself (cf. John 5:23).

b) "Faith toward God"

(1) Acts 2:38—Peter said, "Repent, and be baptized, every one of you, in the name of Jesus Christ for the remission of sins." Repentance comes by faith in Christ; the two concepts are tied together.

(2) Acts 11:17-18—Peter said, "Forasmuch, then, as God gave them the same gift as he did unto us, who believed on the Lord Jesus Christ, what was I, that I could withstand God? When they heard these things, they held their peace, and glorified God, saying, then hath God also to the Gentiles granted repentance unto life." Repentance only comes through faith in the Lord Jesus Christ. The only faith that is acceptable to God is faith in His Son.

The Old Testament taught repentance from dead works and faith toward God. The New Testament teaches repentance toward God and faith in the Lord Jesus Christ, who is the only way to God. The Jewish people the writer addresses in this epistle believed in God, but they were not saved. Their repentance from evil deeds and faith toward God—no matter how sincere it might have been— could not bring them to God without Christ.

c) "The doctrine of baptisms"

The translation "doctrine of baptisms" in the King James Version is misleading. In Hebrews 9:10, the same Greek word (*baptismos*) is translated "washings," so it should be translated the same way here. It is not the usual Greek word for baptism, which is *baptizō*. It may have been that the translators of the Authorized Version assumed this passage was addressed to Christians, in which case the word *baptisms* might have been appropriate. The use of *baptismos* rather than *baptizō* is another strong indication that the passage is not addressed to Christians. The word *baptismos* means "washings" and it refers to the Old Testament washings (cf. Hebrews 9:10). Every Jewish home had a basin by the entrance for family and visitors to use for their many ceremonial cleansings. The writer is encouraging the Hebrews to drop their doctrines of ceremonial cleansing and come to true cleansing.

(1) Ezekiel 36:25-26—Through the prophet God said, "I [will] sprinkle clean water upon you, and ye shall be clean; from all your filthiness, and from all your idols, will I cleanse you. A new heart also will I give you, and a new Spirit will I put within you." God Himself predicted that there would come a day when man would be spiritually cleansed. Cleansings would no longer be physical, symbolic, and temporary. Rather the one final cleansing would be spiritual, real, and permanent.

(2) Titus 3:5—Paul told Titus, "Not by works of righteousness which we have done, but according to his mercy he saved us, by the washing of regeneration, and renewing of the Holy Spirit." The Jewish people needed to abandon the external washings and pursue the real washing that comes in our hearts by faith in Christ.

(3) John 3:5—Jesus told Nicodemus, "Except a man be born of water and of the Spirit, he cannot enter into the Kingdom of God." Jesus was talking about salvation. That is the internal cleansing of which Ezekiel spoke. It would be the only frame of reference Nicodemus could have for understanding Christ's statement since he was the preeminent teacher in Israel (cf. John 3:1). He couldn't have understood that phrase to mean Christian baptism at all because there was no such thing as Christian baptism at that time.

d) "Laying on of hands"

This laying on of hands has nothing to do with the apostolic practices (e.g. Acts 5:18; 6:6; 8:17; 1 Tim. 4:14). Under the Old Covenant, the person who brought an animal sacrifice had to put his hands on it to signify his identification with that sacrifice (Lev. 1:4; 3:8, 13). The writer of Hebrews is saying to forget about the laying on of hands with animal sacrifices, and instead lay hold of Christ by faith. Our identification with Jesus Christ doesn't come by putting our hands on His physical body but by being baptized by the Holy Spirit into the spiritual Body of Christ (1 Cor. 12:13).

e) "Resurrection of the dead"

(1) In the Old Testament

The Old Testament doctrine of resurrection is not clear or complete. We simply learn that men will live after death, and there will be reward for the good and punishment for evil.

(*a*) Job 19:25-27—Job said, "I know that my redeemer liveth, and that he shall stand at the latter day upon the earth; and though after my skin worms destroy this body, yet in my flesh shall I see God, whom I shall see for myself . . . though my heart be consumed within me." He knew he would have a restored body.

(*b*) Daniel 12:2—An angel told Daniel, "Many of those who sleep in the dust of the earth shall awake, some to everlasting life and some to shame and everlasting contempt."

(2) In the New Testament

However, the full doctrine concerning the subject of resurrection blooms in the New Testament.

(*a*) John 11:25—Jesus said, "I am the resurrection and the life." In its fullness, the doctrine of resurrection finds itself in the person of Jesus Christ.

(*b*) 1 Corinthians 15—An entire chapter is devoted to specific details about the resurrection of our bodies.

(c) 1 John 3:2—"It doth not yet appear what we shall be, but we know that, when he shall appear, we shall be like him; for we shall see him as he is."

Why should anyone be content with trying to understand the resurrection from the limited and vague teachings of the Old Testament? The writer of Hebrews is saying that the Jewish people need to come to the full revelation about resurrection truth in the New Testament.

f) "Eternal judgment"

(1) In the Old Testament

Ecclesiastes 12:14 says, "God shall bring every work into judgment, with every secret thing, whether it be good, or whether it be evil." We can learn little more than that concerning final judgment in the Old Testament. But in the New Testament, we are told a great deal about eternal judgment.

(2) In the New Testament

(a) Romans 8:1—Paul said, "There is, therefore, now no condemnation to them who are in Christ Jesus." Believers will not be condemned in the final judgment.

(b) 1 Corinthians 3:12-15—Paul also said, "Now if any man build upon this foundation gold, silver, precious stones, wood, hay, stubble— every man's work shall be made manifest; for the day shall declare it, because it shall be revealed by fire; and the fire shall test every man's work of what sort it is. If any man's work abide which he hath built upon it, he shall receive a reward. If any man's work shall be burned, he shall suffer loss; but he himself shall be saved, yet as by fire." We will stand before the Lord and have our work judged—for reward or for the lack of them— but we ourselves will not be judged.

(c) Matthew 25:46—Matthew said, "These [goats] shall go away into everlasting punishment, but the righteous into life eternal." We also know what is going to happen to unbelievers in the judgment of sheep and goats.

(d) Revelation 20:11-12—John said, "I saw a great white throne, and him that sat on it, from whose face the earth and the heaven fled away, and there was found no place for them. And I saw the dead, small and great, stand before God, and the books were opened; and another book was opened, which is the book of life. And the dead were judged out of those things which were written in the books, according to their works." This is the judgment of the great white throne.

(e) John 5:22—Jesus said, "The father judgeth no man, but hath committed all judgment unto the Son." We know this and much more about judgment from the New Testament.

The point of Hebrews 6:1-2 is that unbelieving Jewish people should go beyond the elementary principles of the Old Covenant and grasp the mature and perfect reality of the New. The Holy Spirit is calling them to leave the ABC's of repentance from dead works for the New Testament teaching of repentance toward God and faith in the Lord Jesus Christ. They're to leave the ABC's of faith toward God for faith in the Person of our Lord Jesus Christ. They're to leave the ABC's of ceremonial washings for the cleansing of the soul by the Word. They're to leave the ABC's of laying hands on the sacrifice for laying hold of the lamb of God by faith. They're to leave the ABC's of the resurrection of the dead for the full and glorious resurrection unto life. And, they're to leave the ABC's of eternal judgment for the full truth of judgment and rewards as revealed in the New Covenant.

The Old Testament is incomplete. It is true, it is of God, and it was a necessary part of His revelation and His plan of salvation, but it is partial revelation only and is not sufficient. Judaism is no longer a valid expression of worship or of obedience to God. It must be abandoned.

3. The need for power (v. 3)

"This will we do, if God permit."

Interpreting this verse is difficult, despite its brevity. It can be seen from two different angles.

a) The writer's perspective

Some interpreters believe the word *we* refers to the writer of Hebrews himself as if he were saying, "I will go on and teach you what you need to know if God permits me."

b) The Lord's perspective

Other interpreters believe the writer is simply identifying himself with those to whom he writes, as if to say, "You will go on to maturity if God permits."

I believe both interpretations could be correct. They are not mutually exclusive and are consistent with the rest of Hebrews. Both service (the writer's going on to teach) and salvation (the readers' going on to maturity in Christ) must be energized by the Holy Spirit if they are to be effective and fruitful. The need for divine enablement is the point of verse 3.

Paul says in 2 Corinthians 3:5, "Not that we are sufficient of ourselves to think anything as of ourselves, but our sufficiency is of God." Perhaps in a similar vein of humility the writer of Hebrews was acknowledging that he had no right to teach spiritual maturity to the Hebrews unless God directed him to. James said, "Come now, ye that say, Today or tomorrow we will go into such a city, and continue there a year, and buy and sell, and get gain; whereas ye know not what shall be on the next day. For what is your life? It is even a vapor that appeareth for a little time, and then vanisheth away. For ye ought to say, if the Lord will, we shall live, and do this, or that" (James 4:13-15). Perhaps applying this to the unbeliever, James was saying that whatever you do is subject to the sovereignty of God. By teacher and seeker alike, God's sovereignty should be recognized (John 6:44).

4. The need for remembrance (vv. 4-5)

"For it is impossible for those who were once enlightened, and have tasted of the heavenly gift, and were made partakers of the Holy Spirit, and have tasted the good word of God, and the powers of the age to come, if they shall fall away, to renew them again unto repentance, seeing they crucify to themselves the Son of God afresh, and put him to an open shame."

That is a serious warning. You had better come to Christ, for if you fall away after having been exposed to the truth, it will be impossible for you to be saved. Some have used this passage to prove that you can lose your salvation. But it is not even addressed to Christians. Those who believe you can lose your salvation have problems with this passage because if it teaches that, then it also teaches that you can't get it back again. Another problem with that view is the multiplicity of other passages in the New Testament that teach the security of salvation (e.g., John 10:27-29; Rom. 5:1-11; Rom. 8:35-39; Phil. 1:6; 1 Pet. 1:3). The writer of Hebrews is speaking to those on the verge of making a commitment to Christ.

The gospel was preached to the Hebrew readers by the apostles. Chapter 2:4 that says they saw the signs, wonders, miracles, and gifts of the Spirit. The Hebrew audience had accepted the gospel intellectually but were close to walking away and returning to Judaism. They were therefore close to being eternally lost because there is no other alternative: You either go on to full knowledge in Christ or you are lost forever. Hebrews 6:4-5 is a classic definition of apostasy.

Because of the seriousness of this passage, many have tried to change the wording to read, "It is *difficult* to repent." But the word is not *difficult*; it is *impossible* (Gk., *adunaton*). The same word occurs in 6:18, 10:4, and 11:6, which all require the translation "impossible." When you come to the point of being convinced about who Christ is—maybe even being a faithful church member—without making a commitment to Him, you are in danger of falling away. And if that is true of you, it is impossible for you to be saved. That is the teaching of the Word of God.

The Hebrews who are being addressed here had five great advantages. They are summarized in verses 4-5:

a) They had been enlightened

To understand what the passage is saying, you must understand what it is *not* saying. It makes no reference whatsoever to salvation. There is no mention of justification, sanctification, the new birth, regeneration, or being born again. None of the normal terminology for salvation is used in this passage. And no term used in this passage is used elsewhere in the New Testament to refer to salvation.

The term "once enlightened" means "to have come to an intellectual perception of truth." It is used in the Septuagint (the Greek translation of the Hebrew Old Testament) to refer to someone who has been given light by knowledge or teaching. It simply means to be mentally aware or to have been instructed in something. It carries no connotation of acceptance or rejection, belief or disbelief.

(1) Matthew 4:16—"The people who sat in darkness saw great light." Jesus fulfilled the prophecy in Isaiah 42:6-7. It does not mean that all the people of Galilee were saved. They were enlightened by having seen Christ and His miracles, but everyone did not believe as a result. The light of the glorious gospel had broken in on their darkness, and their lives could never be the same again. The same thing had happened to those whom the author of Hebrews addresses.

(2) John 1:9—John said Christ "was the true Light, which lighteth every man that cometh into the world." Not all who saw and heard that light were saved. Seeing God's light and accepting it are not the same. Many men have factual information concerning Christ, but not all believe. The lives of all who saw Jesus were permanently affected by the indelible impression He made on them, yet most did not believe in Him (cf. John 12:37-40).

(3) 2 Peter 2:20—Peter said, "For if, after they have escaped the pollutions of the world through the knowledge of the Lord and Savior, Jesus Christ, they are again entangled in it, and overcome, the latter end is worse with them than the beginning." It is better for you to know nothing, than to know the gospel, ignore it, and then finally walk away after having been enlightened.

The same thing had happened to the Jews being addressed in Hebrews 6:1-8. They were enlightened but not saved. They were in danger of losing all opportunity of being saved. They were in danger of becoming apostates because of their continual unbelief. The light that was given to save them could easily become a judgment against them.

b) They had tasted the heavenly gift

There are several things to which "the heavenly gift" could refer. The Holy Spirit is spoken of in Scripture as a heavenly gift, but since He is mentioned in the next verse, this is probably not a reference to Him. Another heavenly gift mentioned in Scripture is salvation (Eph. 2:8). Christ Himself is called the unspeakable gift in 2 Corinthians 9:15. Neither, however, was yet received by the Hebrew audience in view in verse 4. The passage does not say they feasted on the heavenly gift, lived by it, or ate it. They merely tasted it.

(1) John 4:10—Speaking to the woman at the well, "Jesus answered, and said unto her, If thou knowest the gift of God [salvation], and who it is that saith to thee, Give me to drink, thou wouldest have asked of him, and he would have given thee living water." He went on to say that all those who drink living water are truly saved. Tasting is not drinking. Tasting is merely sampling a small portion of something to decide whether you want it. If it does not taste good, you do not drink. But drinking in living water— committing yourself after your first taste—is salvation.

(2) John 6:32, 53—In talking to the Pharisees, "Jesus said unto them, Verily, verily, I say unto you, Moses gave you not that bread from heaven; but my Father giveth you the true bread from heaven. . . . Except ye eat the flesh of the Son of man, and drink his blood, ye have no life in you." Jesus was saying that eternal life comes from eating—not simply tasting—God's gift of salvation in Christ.

One of the pre-salvation ministries of the Holy Spirit is to enable the unsaved to have a taste of the blessings of salvation. But tasting is not the same as eating. The Holy Spirit will give us a taste, but He will not make us eat. The Spirit of God placed the blessing of salvation on the lips of the Hebrews, but they had not yet eaten. The tasting had come from what they

41

saw and heard, as many today have seen the transforming power of Christ and heard the gospel.

c) They were partakers of the Holy Spirit

The Greek word for "partakers" is *metochous*, which
refers to an association. It does not mean these
Hebrews possessed the Holy Spirit; it simply means
they were around when the Holy Spirit was at work.
The same word is used to speak of fellow fishermen
in Luke 5:7 and of Christ in relation to the angels in
Hebrews 1:9. It refers to a common sharing in certain
activities or events.

The term can refer to Christians, as in Hebrews 3:1,
but it can also refer to non-Christians. It is possible to
have an association with the Holy Spirit—to have a
share in what He does—and not be saved. The
Hebrews had heard the Word of God and seen God
bear witness to the diverse miracles and gifts of the
Holy Spirit (Heb. 2:4). They actually took part in what
the Holy Spirit was doing. However, the Bible never
speaks of Christians being associated with the Holy
Spirit. It speaks of the Holy Spirit being within them.

That is seen in the Old Testament economy, for at
that time the Holy Spirit worked through a person
without permanently indwelling the believer. Perhaps like most of the multitudes that Jesus miraculously healed and fed, the Hebrews partook of the
Holy Spirit's power and blessings, but they did not
have His indwelling. They did not possess the Holy
Spirit, nor did the Holy Spirit possess them.

You Cannot Buy the Holy Spirit

Many people would like to benefit from the blessings and
miracles of the Holy Spirit without making a commitment to Him.
A man named Simon Magus in Acts 8:9-25 wanted to buy the
Holy Spirit. He wanted the power of the Holy Spirit but was not
saved. The text says, "There was a certain man, called Simon,
who previously in the same city used sorcery, and bewitched the
people of Samaria, giving out that himself was some great one, to
whom they all gave heed, from the least to the greatest, saying,
this man is the great power of God. And to him they had regard,
because that for a long time he had bewitched them with
sorceries. But when they believed Philip preaching the things
concerning the kingdom of God, and the name of Jesus Christ,

they were baptized, both men and women. Then Simon himself believed also; and when he was baptized, he continued with Philip, and was amazed, beholding the miracles and signs which were done" (vv. 9-13). Verses 18-20 say, "When Simon saw that through laying on of the apostles' hands the Holy Spirit was given, he offered them money, saying, Give me also this power, that on whomsoever I lay hands, he may receive the Holy Spirit. But Peter said unto him, Thy money perish with thee, because thou hast thought that the gift of God may be purchased with money."

Revival had happened in Samaria and this sorcerer had "believed"—the kind of belief akin to Jesus' so-called disciples in John 6:66, which says, "From that time many of his disciples went back, and walked no more with him." John 8:31 says, "Then said Jesus to those Jews who believed on him, If ye continue in my word, then are ye my disciples indeed." Believing is only the beginning. Simon believed in Christ intellectually but only in order to buy the Holy Spirit's power for his own ends. He was even baptized by the disciples as a believer but was not saved. Peter didn't rebuke him as a fellow Christian for he said, "Repent, therefore, of this thy wickedness, and pray God, if perhaps the thought of thine heart may be forgiven thee; for I perceive that thou art in the gall of bitterness, and in the bond of iniquity." Simon was partaking in what the Holy Spirit was doing but he was not for real. You cannot buy the Holy Spirit's power; you must commit your life in obedience to God and allow the Holy Spirit to work through you.

d) They had tasted the good word of God

The Hebrews even had the opportunity to taste the words (Gk., *rhēma*) of God. *Logos*, not *rhēma*, is most often used to refer to God's Word, but *rhēma* best fits the context of the passage. The Hebrews had actually heard and been taught the very speeches (*rhēma*) concerning God and Christ. They were regular attenders in the assembly of the church. As with His heavenly gifts, they had heard God's utterances and sampled them, tasted them, without actually eating—obeying His truths. They could not say with the prophet Jeremiah, "Thy words were found, and I did eat them, and thy word was unto me the joy and rejoicing of mine heart" (Jer. 15:16). They never let the words of God become an actual part of their lives.

Herod Antipas was much like these Hebrews. He enjoyed hearing John the Baptist's preaching, which included accusations directly against him (Mark 6:20). Herod was perplexed but fascinated by that dynamic preacher. He liked to sample the message of God. But when it came time for a decision, he forsook God's man and God's message. Although reluctantly, he agreed to have John beheaded. His taste of God's Word only brought him greater guilt.

The Hebrews had tasted the good Word of God. Every man must taste the Word of God before he accepts it. King David said, "O taste and see that the Lord is good" (Ps. 34:8, NASB). The problem is stopping with the tasting. At first to the Hebrews, the first preaching of the gospel was sweet and tasted good. But as it lingered in their mouth, they grew dull and became sluggish and indifferent. They did not chew or swallow it, much less digest it. Their spiritual taste buds became insensitive and unresponsive.

e) They had tasted the powers of the age to come

The age to come is the future kingdom of God. The Hebrews had been exposed to the same miraculous power that will come when Jesus brings in His earthly kingdom. They had tasted it, witnessing signs, wonders, and miracles. The more they saw, the more their guilt increased. They were like those who saw Jesus Himself perform miracles. It is hard to understand the hatred and unbelief of those who saw Lazarus risen from the dead (John 11:1-44), and the blind, deaf, and dumb healed (Matt. 4:23). They will all stand guilty before God at the great white throne judgment because they saw but did not believe.

The author of Hebrews is saying "You have had the whole Old Testament revelation with all its basic elements. And in this age, you've been enlightened, tasted of the gift of salvation, partook of what the Spirit was doing in your midst, tasted the good speeches and utterances concerning God and saw miracle upon miracle. But you're in danger if you don't repent."

5. The need for a response (v. 6)

"If they shall fall away, [it is impossible] to renew them again unto repentance."

44

a) The apostasy

The Greek word for "fall away" is *parapesontas* and is only used here in the New Testament. Summarized, the warning is: "You had better come to Christ now, for if you fall away, it will be impossible for you to come again to the point of repentance." The Hebrews were at the best possible point of repentance—full knowledge. To fall back from that would be fatal. That class of people is defined in Hebrews 3:12 as those who "[depart] from the living God" (cf. 2 Pet. 2:20-22).

b) The attitude

Many who say this warning passage is dealing with Christians base their assumptions on the word *renew* in verse 6. The word means "to restore" or "to bring back to an original condition." What was the Hebrews' original condition? They had heard the gospel and were excited about it. They had moved away from Judaism right to the edge of Christianity. They had even moved toward repentance but had turned back to their old ways. There was nothing else God could do. If they fell away now, they did so with an evil heart of unbelief in spite of full revelation. They would be departing from the living God, and there was no hope they would ever be restored to the place where repentance would be a natural response.

c) The action

What kept the Hebrews from being repentant? They had crucified "to themselves the Son of God afresh and put Him to an open shame" (v. 6). They couldn't repent because as far as they were concerned, the Son of God deserved to be crucified. Regardless of what they might have professed openly and publicly, they took their stand with the crucifiers. The word translated "afresh" simply means "to lift up in crucifixion." The Hebrews were lifting up Jesus Christ for crucifixion.

Even with all the evidence, they decided that Christ was not the true Messiah. They had turned and gone back to Judaism. To them Jesus was an impostor and deceiver who got exactly what was coming to Him.

By putting Him "to an open shame," they were declaring openly that Jesus was guilty as charged.

Salvation to an apostate becomes impossible, for when he rejects full revelation, he is incurably anti-God and deserves the hottest of hell. He takes his place with Judas, who walked and talked with God incarnate, yet finally rejected Him. Hebrews 10:29 says, "How much sorer punishment, suppose ye, shall he be thought worthy, who hath trodden under foot the Son of God, and hath counted the blood of the covenant, with which he was sanctified, an unholy thing, and hath done despite unto the Spirit of grace?"

It is dangerously self-deceptive for a person to think he is safe by staying on the sidelines or by thinking himself tolerant of the gospel simply because he does not outwardly oppose it. If you don't come to Jesus Christ, you eventually will go away from Him. It may not be, and often is not, a conscious decision against Christ. But it *is* a decision and it *is* against Christ. And when you finally reject Christ, you again place Him on the cross and put the Lord forever out of your reach.

6. The need for an illustration (vv. 7-8)

The writer closes the passage with an illustration describing those who ultimately reject the Messiah: "The earth, which drinketh in the rain that cometh often upon it, and bringeth forth herbs fit for them by whom it is tilled, receiveth blessing from God; but that which beareth thorns and briers is rejected, and is near unto cursing, whose end is to be burned" (vv. 7-8). This illustration shows that verses 1-6 are directed toward unbelievers. The writer is saying that all who hear the gospel are like the earth. The gospel seed is planted and some of the growth is beautiful, good, and productive. That represents the goodness and blessings of God. At other times though, with the same message, some growth is false, spurious, and unproductive (v. 8). It has come from the same ground and the same water but has become worthless. Thorns and briers are the result. It has rejected the life offered it and becomes good only for burning. The picture shows that as God's gracious gospel falls on men, it brings forth fruit with some but with others it brings forth thorns. I pray to God that when the rain of the gospel of Jesus Christ falls on you, it brings forth fruit.

Focusing on the Facts

1. What were the Jewish people warned about repeatedly in the book of Hebrews (see pp. 26-27)?
2. The term _____ in Hebrews 5:13 describes _____ (see p. 27).
3. True or false: People can go to church for years and hear the gospel over and over again, even being faithful church members, and never really make a commitment to Jesus Christ (see p. 27).
4. What is the progression for those who ultimately reject salvation (see p. 28)?
5. Understanding the word _____ and the phrase _____ is the crux of interpreting Hebrews 6:1-8 (see p. 28).
6. What is the writer asking the Hebrews to do in Hebrews 6:1 (see p. 30)?
7. What is the writer of Hebrews commanding the Jewish people to do (see p. 31)?
8. What did the writer mean when he asked his readers to "go on to perfection" (see p. 31)?
9. What does the "repentance from dead works" refer to? How does it differ from the concept of repentance in the New Testament? Support your answer with Scripture (see pp. 32-33).
10. What is the second Old Testament doctrine that the writer speaks of and how does it differ from the New Testament doctrine (see p. 33)?
11. Explain the difference between baptisms and washings (see pp. 33-34).
12. How is the term "laying on of hands" in Hebrews 6:2 different from the apostolic practice (see p. 35)?
13. How does the Old Testament describe the resurrection of the dead? Explain how the New Testament helps to clarify the doctrine of resurrection (see pp. 35-36).
14. What does the Old Testament tell us about eternal judgment? What light does the New Testament shed on the subject (see pp. 36-37)?
15. The point of Hebrews 6:1-2 is that _____ Jewish people should completely let go of the elementary symbols of the Old Covenant and take hold of the _____ and perfect reality of the_____ (see p. 37).
16. True or False: The Old Testament is complete. The New Testament is simply an added feature of the Old Testament saying basically the same thing. Explain (see p. 37).
17. From what two perspectives can verse 3 be taken? Explain them (see pp. 38-39).

18. Can a person lose his salvation? Support your answer with Scripture (see p. 39).
19. Hebrews 6:4-5 is a classic definition of _____ (see p. 39).
20. Explain what it means to be enlightened about the gospel, giving examples from Scripture (see pp. 39-40).
21. What does it mean to have "tasted of the heavenly gift"? Explain your answer with biblical examples (see p. 41).
22. Must someone who is a "partaker of the Holy Spirit" be a Christian? Explain (see p. 42).
23. What do the phrases "tasted the good word of God" and "the powers of the age to come" refer to (see pp. 43-44)?
24. What does the word *renew* signify in verse 6 (see p. 45)?
25. By neglecting to respond to Christ, what were the Hebrews in actuality doing (Heb. 6:6; see pp. 45-46)?
26. What is the point of the illustration in verses 7-8 (see pp. 46-47)?

Pondering the Principles

1. Maturity is something everyone should desire. It is not an option for the Christian. There is no such thing as remaining static in the Christian life. You are either progressing or regressing. Are you maturing in your Christian life? Are you in a state of progression or regression? The apostle Paul calls us to examine ourselves in 2 Corinthians 13:5. Study the following lists to see if they describe the pattern of your life: 1 Corinthians 6:9-10, Galatians 5:19-21, and Revelation 21:8. If they do, confess your sin to God and ask for His forgiveness.

2. Many people do not understand what repentance means. After having read the lesson, describe in your own words what repentance means. Explain how the Old Testament concept differs from that in the New. After you have come up with a good working definition, look up 2 Corinthians 7:9-10 and describe the difference between sorrow or guilt and true repentance. Then ask yourself this: Am I truly repentant over my sinfulness or am I just sorrowful? If you said you were sorrowful, repent right now to God over your sinfulness. Ask Him to give you a new heart and make you the kind of person He wants you to be.

3. One of the most sorrowful passages in the Bible is Hebrews 6:4-6. It describes those who had been given full revelation from God,

yet still continued to reject Him. Do you know someone who knows the reality of the gospel of Christ, yet continues to reject it by failing to make a definite commitment to Christ? Share Hebrews 6:4-6 with him, explaining the seriousness of what he is doing. Share with him that unless he acts soon, it may be impossible for him to come to Christ.

3
The Tragedy of Rejecting Full Revelation—Part 3

Outline

Introduction

Review
I. The Warning to Non-Christians (5:10—6:8)
   A. The Problem (5:10-14)
   B. The Solution (6:1-8)
      1. The need for maturity (v. 1a)
      2. The need for a new foundation (vv. 1b-2)
      3. The need for power (v. 3)
      4. The need for remembrance (vv. 4-5)
      5. The need for response (v. 6)
      6. The need for an illustration (vv. 7-8)

Lesson
II. The Word to Christians (vv. 9-12)
   A. The Evaluation (v. 9)
      1. Defining the terms for the brethren
      2. Delineating the truth about salvation
   B. The Examination (v. 10)
      1. The fruit determines the reality of salvation
         a) 1 Thessalonians 1:3
         b) Galatians 5:6
      2. The fruit determines the reason for service
         a) 2 Corinthians 5:14
         b) Romans 1:5
         c) 3 John 7
         d) John 21:17
      3. The fruit determines the resource for service
         a) The motive
         b) The methods
         c) The ministers

C. The Emulation (vv. 11-12)

Conclusion

Introduction

Hebrews 5:10—6:8 is about spiritual maturity. It is one of the so-called warning passages in Hebrews that relates not to believers but to unbelievers. Because of the depth and richness of this particular portion of Scripture, it needs to be studied in minute detail. The two previous chapters have dealt with the tragedy of Hebrews who had rejected the full revelation that God had given them concerning Jesus Christ.

Review

I. THE WARNING TO NON-CHRISTIANS (5:10—6:8; see pp. 13-22, 27-47)

The gospel had been preached to the Jewish community by the apostles and prophets (cf. 2:3) and the writer was actually dealing with a second generation of hearers.

In coming the Christ, the believers had to make a complete break with Judaism. Upon receiving Jesus Christ they were immediately ostracized from Jewish society. The cost was heavy, the pressure was great, and the persecution intense. The book of Hebrews was written primarily to Christians who had made a clean break from Judaism to receive Jesus Christ as Savior and Lord.

There was a second group of Jewish people addressed in the book of Hebrews, and they were in danger of missing salvation because of their desire to hang on to some of the Old Testament patterns without recognizing their fulfillment in the New. The writer of Hebrews says repeatedly, "Let go of Old Testament patterns pointing to Christ and embrace Him instead." As Paul says in Colossians 2:10, "Ye are complete in him." The author then encouraged them to make a complete break with the patterns of the Old Covenant and come to the New.

Throughout the book of Hebrews are warnings to this group of people. They had been intellectually convinced of the validity of Christianity but had not made a commitment. They had turned away from Judaism enough to have moved in with the Christian community, and might have even professed to be true Christians.

But the fact is they were not. The warnings occur in the following portions of Hebrews: 2:1-4; 3:7—4:13; 5:10—6:8; 10:26-31; and 12:25-29. They were designed for those who had gone through all the stages preliminary to salvation but had never experienced it. They were in danger of falling away to the point of no return.

A. The Problem (5:10-14; see pp. 13-22)

The Hebrews were spiritually ignorant and were gradually growing harder and more calloused to the things of God. They could no longer discern between good and evil (5:11-14).

B. The Solution (6:1-8; see pp. 27-47)

1. The need for maturity (v. 1a; see pp. 28-31)

The writer of Hebrews gave the solution to their predicament beginning in verse 1 of chapter 6: "Therefore, leaving the principles of the doctrine of Christ, let us go on unto perfection." They needed to leave the Old Covenant and come to maturity in the full revelation of the New Covenant.

2. The need for a new foundation (vv. 1b-2; see pp. 31-37)

The readers of the epistle are exhorted to go beyond "repentance from dead works" and "faith toward God" (turning to faith in Christ instead), "the doctrine of washings" (ceremonial washings), "laying on of hands" (to identify with a sacrifice), "the resurrection of the dead" (an undefined doctrine in the Old Testament), and "eternal judgment" (not fully developed in the Old Testament). The solution is to leave the basic elements of Judaism and come to Jesus Christ.

3. The need for power (v. 3; see pp. 37-38)

The power to accomplish the task of learning about the New Covenant is in verse 3: "And this will we do, if God permit." The writer was acknowledging that anything we do is accomplished only in the permissive will of God. Divine enablement alone could allow the Hebrews to go on to maturity.

4. The need for remembrance (vv. 4-5; see pp. 38-44)

The heart of the passage is the warning in verses 4-5: "It is impossible for those who were once enlightened, and have tasted of the heavenly gift, and were made partakers of the Holy Spirit, and have tasted the good word of

God, and the powers of the age to come, if they shall fall away, to renew them again unto repentance, seeing they crucify to themselves the Son of God afresh, and put him to an open shame."

The Hebrews had come close to the point of making a decision for Christ with full revelation from God but were now close to falling away into a state of permanent disbelief. They were enlightened but not saved; they had tasted but not eaten; they had partaken of the Holy Spirit but did not possess Him. Hebrews 6:1-8 should not be interpreted as referring to Christians. Christians cannot fall away (cf. Jude 24).

5. The need for a response (v. 6; see pp. 44-46)

Anyone who rejects Christ stands with those who put Him on trial. Such a person is passing the guilty verdict and identifying with the crucifiers.

The Unforgivable Sin

In Matthew 12 Jesus heals a paralytic on the Sabbath. Verses 24-28, 31 say, "When the Pharisees heard it, they said, this fellow doth not cast out demons, but by Beelzebub, the prince of demons. And Jesus knew their thoughts, and said unto them, Every kingdom divided against itself is brought to desolation; and every city or house divided against itself shall not stand. And if Satan cast out Satan, he is divided against himself; how shall then his kingdom stand? And if I, by Beelzebub, cast out demons, by whom do your sons cast them out? Therefore, they shall be your judges. But if I cast out demons by the Spirit of God, then the kingdom of God is come unto you. . . . Wherefore, I say unto you, all manner of sin and blasphemy shall be forgiven men; but the blasphemy against the Holy Spirit shall not be forgiven men."

Do you know what it means to blaspheme the Holy Spirit? To actually see the works of Christ—to have that full revelation—yet attribute them to Satan. It is seeing all there is to see and still walking away, saying the very opposite of what is true. For that, there is no forgiveness. Jesus says in verse 32, "Whosoever speaketh a word against the Son of man, it shall be forgiven him; but whosoever speaketh against the Holy Spirit, it shall not be forgiven him, neither in this age, neither in the age to come." The blasphemy of the Holy Spirit is a sin that is isolated to the period when Jesus was on the earth, because that was the only time when men could physically see His works and attribute them to

Satan. It will be possible for this sin to be committed when Christ is present on earth during the millennial kingdom.

In the meantime, men can commit a sin that is similar, and that is receiving full revelation from God, yet turning their backs on Him forever. By so doing, they have sentenced themselves to eternal doom.

6. The need for an illustration (vv. 7-8; see pp. 46-47)

The writer of Hebrews gives an illustration in verses 7-8 that shows the difference between those who profess Christ and those who actually possess Him: "The earth, which drinketh in the rain that cometh often upon it, and bringeth forth herbs fit for them by whom it is tilled, receiveth blessing from God; but that which beareth thorns and briers is rejected, and is near unto cursing, whose end is to be burned." The writer is saying that the grace of God rains upon the earth—the earth representing all types of men. Some men hear the gospel, believe the message, and bring forth fruit, but some men bring forth nothing but thorns and briers that are cast in the fire and burned. The distinction is this: The Hebrews had heard and seen the full revelation of God. Some believed and brought forth fruit while others did not and brought forth thorns and briers.

The thorns and briers are not necessarily evil deeds but the works of self-righteousness. He is contrasting two kinds of religion: the religion of divine accomplishment, which is based on all that God has done in Christ, and the religion of human achievement, which is based on what man does to secure his own salvation. The only way man will ever bring forth fruit acceptable to God is to abide in Christ (cf. John 15:5).

Lesson

II. THE WORD TO CHRISTIANS (vv. 9-12)

"But, beloved, we are persuaded better things of you, and things that accompany salvation, though we thus speak. For God is not unrighteous to forget your work and labor of love, which ye have shown toward his name, in that ye have ministered to the saints, and do minister. And we desire that every one of you do show the same diligence to the full assurance of hope unto the end; that ye be not slothful, but followers of them who through faith and patience inherit the promises."

After the writer of Hebrews gives the severest of warnings, he proceeds in verses 9-12 to give the most loving of appeals. He was hoping earnestly that the unbelievers he had been warning so forcefully would not fall away. His approach was to encourage them to be imitators of the true Christians in their midst. That is a consistent pattern in Scripture. The apostle Paul says to the Corinthians, "Be imitators of me, just as I also am of Christ" (1 Cor. 11:1, NASB). He also said this to Timothy: "Let no man despise thy youth, but be thou an example [to] the believers, in word, in conduct, in love, in Spirit, in faith, in purity" (1 Tim. 4:12).

To those who were sluggish and in danger of falling away, the writer of Hebrews says, "Let me introduce you to the Christians in your midst. Look at their lives and pattern yourselves after them. Follow those who through faith and patience inherit the promises." In contrast to the non-Christians who have been the object of the writer's message in 5:10—6:8, he shows them the true believers in verses 9-12, who stand as an example of what the unbelievers ought to be.

Both readers had the same Jewish background. They had come to the same point of repentance. They both had the very same revelation from God. The difference is only that one group had gone a step further by totally committing themselves to Jesus Christ. That is a profound difference. My dad is fond of saying, "The same sun that hardens the clay, melts the wax." When we come to verses 9-12, the writer's perspective changes: he has been addressing non-Christians but now addresses Christians.

A. The Evaluation (v. 9)

"But, beloved, we are persuaded better things of you, and things that accompany salvation, though we thus speak."

The writer here gives a brief word to the believers who are to be imitated. We know that because he says "beloved," a term that is never used in Scripture to refer to unbelievers. Note the pronoun used to refer to the unbelievers in verse 4: "It is impossible for *those* [to be renewed unto repentance]" (emphasis added). In verse 9, however, the pronoun *you* is used, indicating that the writer is addressing a different group of people. Here is the final proof that those in Hebrews 5:10—6:8 were not true Christians. The bearers of thorns and briers in verses 7-8 were rejected, but the beloved of verse 9 were not.

Those addressed here are like those in Hebrews 10:39: "But we are not of them who draw back unto perdition, but of them that believe to the saving of the soul." Both groups came to the point of decision, but one group drew back into perdition while the other believed and were saved. The believers mentioned in verses 9-12 are said to have love in verse 10, hope in verse 11, and faith in verse 12. This forms the triad of Christians virtues that Paul mentions in 1 Corinthians 13:13. Faith, hope, and love characterize a true believer.

1. Defining the terms for the brethren

   The Greek word for "beloved" (*agapētoi*) expresses the highest form of love in a relationship. It is used sixty-one times in the New Testament. The first nine times it is used, it is used of God the Father in speaking of Christ, His beloved Son. In the rest of the New Testament, whether referring to Jews or Gentiles, it is used primarily to refer to believers. *Agapē* love is the beautiful and unique bond of fellowship between believers. Commentator Arthur Pink observed, "I cannot really love a brother with the Gospel-love, which is required of me, unless I have a well-grounded persuasion that he is a brother" (*An Exposition of Hebrews*, vol. 1 [Grand Rapids: Baker, 1954], p. 325). The writer of Hebrews refers to unbelieving Jews as "brethren" in a racial sense but never as "beloved." *Agapē* love is reserved for those who know Christ personally.

2. Delineating the truth about salvation

   The writer says, "We are persuaded" (v. 9). The phrase is used in a legal sense to refer to someone who examined a case, gathered all the evidence, and then said, "I'm convinced." The writer is saying, "I have considered the evidence and have come to the settled conclusion that you are for real." The evidence was their faith, hope, and love—the traits that accompany salvation.

   The New Testament is rich in its use of the terms for salvation. The word *salvation* itself and its derivatives are used some fifty times in the New Testament. It speaks of our deliverance from danger, death, hell, Satan, and sin.

What are the things that accompany salvation according to the writer of Hebrews?

a) Hebrews 5:11—Salvation is not infancy but maturity.

b) Hebrews 5:12—Salvation is not milk but solid food.

c) Hebrews 5:13—Salvation is not inexperience in righteousness but perfect righteousness.

d) Hebrews 6:1—Salvation is not repentance from dead works but repentance toward God and faith in our Lord Jesus Christ.

e) Hebrews 6:1—Salvation is not faith in God apart from Christ but faith in Christ as God.

f) Hebrews 6:2—Salvation is not external ceremonial religion but internal regeneration and transformation.

g) Hebrews 6:2—Salvation is not repeated identification with sacrifices but a once-for-all identification with Jesus Christ.

h) Hebrews 6:2—Salvation is not unclear definitions of resurrection and eternal judgment but the full revelation of our blessed hope (Titus 2:13).

i) Hebrews 6:4—Salvation is not simply being enlightened but being made new creatures in Christ.

j) Hebrews 6:4—Salvation is not simply tasting salvation but feasting on it completely.

k) Hebrews 6:4—Salvation is not simply partaking of the Holy Spirit but being indwelt by Him in all His fullness.

l) Hebrews 6:5—Salvation is not simply tasting God's word but drinking it up.

m) Hebrews 6:5—Salvation is not simply seeing a miracle but being one.

Those are the characteristics that accompany salvation. The "better things" the writer speaks of in verse 9 are set in contrast to the traits characterizing the unbelievers.

The writer ends verse 9 by saying, "Though thus we speak." This is something of an apology to the Christian reader who had been reading through the awful warning passage, encouraging them not to lose heart. To the Christian, the writer says, "Don't think my warning to the unbelievers refers to you. I put it here because I know they're in your midst." Only Jesus Christ knows who is for real and who isn't, and He will reveal that in the last day (Matt. 13:24-30). The writer, however, wouldn't be able to pick them all out by name.

B. The Examination (v. 10)

"God is not unrighteous to forget your work and labor of love, which ye have shown toward his name, in that ye have ministered to the saints, and do minister."

God knows who are really His and who are faithful. He will not forget His own or their work for Him. Our names are securely in His book of life. Our salvation is not lost, and our rewards will not be forgotten.

Many Christians today are shaken when they hear God's message of judgment. They experience times of anguish and doubt, fearing they might lose their salvation. They do not know what it is to rest in the finished work of Christ and in their positional standing in Christ.

After Malachi had given his severe warning of judgment, many of the faithful believers apparently were worried that it applied to them. The prophet said, "They that feared the Lord spoke often one to another; and the Lord hearkened, and heard it, and a book of remembrance was written before him for them that feared the Lord, and that thought upon his name. And they shall be mine, saith the Lord of hosts" (Mal. 3:16-17). Later in chapter 4 the Lord says, "The day cometh, that shall burn like an oven, and all the proud, yea, and all that do wickedly, shall be stubble; and the day that cometh shall burn them up, saith the Lord of hosts, that it shall leave them neither root nor branch. But unto you that fear my name shall the Sun of righteousness arise with healing in his wings" (vv. 1-2). God always knows His own. The sovereignty of God secures us.

1. The fruit determines the reality of salvation

Many have said Hebrews 6:10 says you must work for your salvation. (They point out it says God won't forget our works, not our faith.) But if that were true, it would contradict what other Scriptures teach (e.g. Eph. 2:8-9; Titus 3:5). The writer is saying that in a congregation with wheat and tares who are all claiming to have faith, the only way to tell the difference is by their good works. A Christian's works are not what saved him or what keeps him saved, but they do give evidence of his salvation. As James tells us, "Faith without works is dead" (James 2:18, 26). You demonstrate your faith by your works and I'll believe your faith is real, for Paul said, "If any man be in Christ, he is a new creation" (2 Cor. 5:17). God is not so unfair and insensitive that He fails to see the works of love His beloved children perform on His behalf. He clearly sees the fruit of our righteousness.

In the statement "labor of love," the term "labor" doesn't appear in the best manuscripts, so the verse could be read this way: "God is not unrighteous to forget your work of love."

a) 1 Thessalonians 1:3—Paul said, "Remembering without ceasing your work of faith, and labor of love." The reason Paul knew the Thessalonian Christians were for real was that he could look at their lives and see the fruits of genuine salvation.

b) Galatians 5:6—Although in a different context, Paul said, "In Jesus Christ neither circumcision availeth anything, nor uncircumcision, but faith which worketh by love." Do you know how you can tell if your faith is real? If genuine love is the result of your faith.

2. The fruit determines the reason for service

Service to the brethren is also evidence of salvation. But an even more significant evidence is love "toward his name" (Heb. 6:10). God knows when our service is truly for His glory by whether it is done out of love for His name—for who He is. Do you know how to express your love for God? Serve the saints. The writer says the Hebrew Christians "ministered to the saints, and do minister" (v. 10). They ministered not primarily because they loved the saints but because they loved God. The key to real service is a burning love for the Lord.

a) 2 Corinthians 5:14—Paul said, "The love of Christ constraineth us." People are not always lovable, but we love them because we love God (cf. 1 John 5:2).

b) Romans 1:5—Paul said, "By whom we have received grace and apostleship, for obedience to the faith among all nations, for his name." What does the name of God mean? It means all that He is. To love

God's name means to have a passionate love for all that He is.

c) 3 John 7—John said, "Because for his name's sake they went forth." The church in view here ministered because they loved God.

d) John 21:17—Jesus first asked Peter, "Simon, son of Jonah, lovest thou me?" Then He said, "Feed my sheep." Jesus didn't ask Peter if he loved men; He asked if he loved *Him*.

Your service to Jesus Christ must be based on an overwhelming love for Him. You will never properly love men until you properly love Him. Loving the name of the Lord is proof positive that your faith is the real thing. The faithful believers to whom Hebrews was primarily addressed loved the name of the Lord. And they were ministering to each other because they loved their Lord. We hear a great deal about loving and ministering to the Body of Christ, but the genuineness and effectiveness of the ministry we do have is directly related to the love we have for Christ. The more we love God, the more we will want to do His will. We shouldn't be concerned with trying to invent love for people, for it should be an overflow from our love for God.

3. The fruit determines the resource for service

   a) The motive

   Keeping God as our focus and resource gives us the desire and ability to love others. Verse 10 says, "Ye have ministered to the saints, and do minister." Their ministry kept going and going. They were not resting on the laurels of past ministry, for it kept on going. The word *minister* is the same Greek word from which we get the word *deacon*. It simply means to serve. The believers were serving each other through their spiritual gifts (cf. Rom. 12:3-8; 1 Cor. 12:8-11; 1 Pet. 4:10-11). Whether your gift is counseling, showing mercy, helping, or teaching, it should be used because you love Him.

   b) The methods

   Our ministry to one another involves praying for one another (Eph. 6:18), rebuking each other when we sin and seeking to restore the sinning brother in love

(Gal. 6:1), confessing our sins to one another (James 5:16), forgiving one another (Eph. 4:32), bearing one another's burdens (Gal. 6:2), caring for the weaker brother (1 Thess. 5:14), and giving to meet the needs of the saints (Rom. 12:13). All those things must be generated by our love for Jesus Christ. The Christian life can be boiled down to one thing: the measure of your love for the Lord. How preoccupied are you with His name? Do you have a lofty, exalted view of who He is and an overwhelming and passionate love for Him? When we love our Lord like that, then we'll be able to love each other as we should.

c) The ministers

The writer refers to the believers as saints in verse 10. All true Christians are saints (Gk., *hagios*), meaning "holy ones" (cf. 1 Cor. 1:2). The writer is speaking of our identity in Christ. We are righteous before God because of our standing in Jesus Christ. Being a saint has nothing to do with one's degree of spiritual maturity or rank. It refers to any person who is saved—set apart by God for Himself in His Son Jesus Christ.

The proof that the Hebrews addressed in 6:9-12 were true believers was their loving, faithful, and continuing ministry to fellow believers. The greatest gift you can give God is your love and service to fellow believers. Don't say you love God and have no use for a fellow Christian. That is why the apostle John says, "He that saith he is in the light, and hateth his brother, is in darkness" (1 John 2:9).

C. The Emulation (vv. 11-12)

"And we desire that every one of you do show the same diligence to the full assurance of hope unto the end; that ye be not slothful, but followers of them who through faith and patience inherit the promises."

Having determined that these are the true believers, the writer then uses them as an example to the unbelievers. He says, "Look at the beloved and follow the kind of pattern they're setting. We want you all to come to the same full assurance of hope to the end. We don't want you to fall away and have no hope."

The only people who really have hope are those who have a relationship with Jesus Christ (Rom. 12:10-12). There is no hope apart from Jesus Christ. The writer says, "We desire that every one of you do show the same diligence" (v. 11). "Diligence" is the Greek word *spoudē*, which means "speed" or "haste." He's saying that the unbelievers needed to be speedy in coming to the full assurance of hope. Salvation is an instantaneous experience, and it should not be postponed (2 Cor. 6:2). *Spoudē* can also refer to terror-stricken speed. The writer is saying, "If you don't quickly come to Jesus Christ, you're going to fall away in ultimate disaster."

The writer then says, "Be not slothful" (v. 12). The King James Version does not translate that phrase correctly, because "slothful" is the same word translated "dull" in 5:11. And it should be here. He goes through the whole cycle of the argument and comes back to warning them not to be dull of hearing.

The Greek word for "followers" is *mimētai*, from which we get the English word *mimic*. The writer is saying to the unbelievers, "Be mimics of those who through faith and patient endurance of persecution inherit the promises."

Conclusion

If you have come to the point of decision regarding Jesus Christ, yet are putting it off, you are in a dangerous position. You will find that the longer you reject, the harder your heart will become. You are in danger of falling away forever. Because you've rejected the full revelation that God has given, He can't give you any more revelation. If you are not a Christian, I pray that you'll not reject the Lord Jesus Christ a moment longer.

Focusing on the Facts

1. What warning does the writer of Hebrews give (see p. 52)?
2. What was the situation surrounding the first generation of Jewish believers in this community (see p. 52)?
3. What are the major groups addressed in Hebrews (see p. 52)?
4. Where do the warning passages occur in Hebrews, and what do they warn unbelievers about (see p. 53)?
5. What is the unforgivable sin? Can the unforgivable sin be committed today? Explain (see pp. 54-55).
6. The only way man will ever bring forth fruit acceptable to God is to _____ in _____ (John 15:5; see p. 55).

7. Whom is the writer of Hebrews addressing in 6:9-12 (see p. 56)?
8. What is the main difference between the two groups the writer addresses in Hebrews (see p. 56)?
9. What is the triad of Christians' virtues and how does it relate to Hebrews 6:10-12 (1 Cor. 13:13; see p. 57)?
10. What is the difference between the terms *brethren* and *beloved* (see p. 57)?
11. Can a Christian lose his salvation? Must a Christian work to keep his salvation? Support your answer with Scripture (see pp. 58-59).
12. What is more significant than love for your fellow man (see p. 59)
13. What is your responsibility in ministering to the Body of Christ (see p. 60)?
14. The Christian life can be boiled down to one thing and that is the measure of your _____ for the Lord (see p. 62).
15. Are all Christians saints or is that description reserved for super-Christians? Explain (see p. 62).
16. Give proof that Hebrews 6:9-12 is directed to believers (see p. 62)?
17. True or False: The only people who really have hope are those who have a _____ with _____ (see pp. 62-63).
18. What kind of diligence was the writer of Hebrews calling for in verse 10 (see p. 63)?
19. What is the writer's final command to the unbelievers in verse 12 (see p. 63)?

Pondering the Principles

1. The issue in Hebrews 5:10—6:12 is spiritual maturity. But before you can mature spiritually, you must start by beginning a relationship with Jesus Christ. Note how salvation is illustrated by the contrasts listed on page 58. Study the illustrations and over the next two weeks, take each of those thirteen contrasts and examine yourself to see whether your salvation is genuine (2 Cor. 13:5). Ask God to confirm your salvation based on the consistency of those traits in your life.

2. Hebrews 6:10 talked about the believers' love for the saints. The writer was encouraged by their continuing ministry of love and faithfulness because of their love for Jesus Christ. Does a genuine love for the Lord motivate your love for fellow believers? Study 1 John 2:9-11 and 5:2-3 and ask God to love others through you.

4
The Securities of God's Promise

Outline

Introduction
A. You Can't Trust in Earthly Things
   1. Relationships
   2. Religion
B. You Can Trust in the Lord
   1. Jeremiah trusted the Lord
   2. Solomon trusted the Lord
   3. David trusted the Lord
   4. Abraham trusted the Lord
      a) The courage of Abraham
         (1) Romans 4
            (a) His faith
            (b) His race
            (c) His age
         (2) James 2:23
      b) The character of Abraham
         (1) He turned from false gods
         (2) He obeyed God's commands
            (a) He was willing to go to Canaan
            (b) He was willing to sacrifice Isaac

Lesson
I. God's Person (vv. 13-15)
   A. He Cannot Lie (v. 13)
      1. His Word
      2. His promise
      3. His gift
   B. He Cannot Lose (vv. 14-15)
      1. Abraham's doubt
      2. Abraham's devotion

II. God's Purpose (v. 14)
    A. God's Unfolding Plan for the World
        1. After the Fall of man
        2. After the Flood on the earth
        3. After the fall of the Tower
    B. God's Unconditional Promise to Abraham
        1. The channel
        2. The choosing
        3. The covenant
    C. God's Unfolding Purpose for Israel
    D. God's Unalterable Program for Mankind
        1. The security of Israel
        2. The security of the believer
            a) Ephesians 1:3-5
            b) Romans 8:28-30
III. God's Pledge (vv. 13*b*, 16-18)
    A. Man's Custom (v. 16)
    B. God's Concession (v. 17)
        1. The pledge of the Holy Spirit
        2. The promise of the Holy Spirit
    C. God's Character (v. 18)
        1. The encouragement He gives
        2. The hope He gives
            a) 1 Timothy 1:1
            b) Colossians 1:5
IV. God's Priest (vv. 19-20)
    A. The Anchor (v. 19)
    B. The Assurance (v. 20)

Introduction

    A. You Can't Trust in Earthly Things

        1. Relationships

There used to be a television program called, "Who Can You Trust?" That is an important question. In our age, we are well on our way to trusting no one. Many have developed a psychosis of distrust, commonly known as the credibility gap. Young people are being taught not to trust anyone but themselves and are learning by first-hand experience that trust is an elusive virtue. Promises often mean little or nothing. A person's word today can seldom be counted on. Lying has become the norm in much of society. The world is full of liars. The Bible says that "the whole world lies in the power of the evil one" (1 John 5:19, NASB). Jesus said that the evil one—the devil—is the father of lies (John 8:44).

2. Religion

In the midst of the confusion that lying and distrust always brings, people are looking for something or someone to trust. They search for something they can bank their lives on. Many put their trust in religion. A person might spend their entire life searching for peace in religion only to find that it never produces real purpose or satisfaction. They may spend years praying to a particular saint, only to find out that someone made a mistake because his saint was not really canonized. Some put their trust in self-proclaimed healers. A mother took her young son to one of those so-called healers in the hope of having his crippled legs straightened. She was told to take off her son's braces and never to put them on him again. A few weeks later, after much pain, emergency surgery was done to save the boy's legs from amputation.

False evangelists have always been around to take people's hearts, trust, and money. Not too many years ago a Los Angeles minister conducted a television campaign ostensibly to raise money for missionary work. After raising a considerable sum, he left town and disappeared. People go to churches that claim to teach about Jesus Christ and His glory but in reality teach doctrines that are utterly contrary to what He taught. They learn nothing about the Christ of Scripture. False teachers, who are both deceived and deceiving, abound (2 Tim. 3:13). There are preachers with high academic credentials from prestigious seminaries who teach philosophies and theology that are totally unbiblical and heretical. So who can you trust?

B. You Can Trust in the Lord

Without being pessimistic or cynical, the Christian knows that the only one who can be trusted without reservation is God.

1. Jeremiah trusted the Lord

The prophet Jeremiah said, "Trust not in lying words" (Jer. 7:4). Trusting in the Lord with all your heart is the only answer in today's trustless world.

2. Solomon trusted the Lord

   Proverbs 29:25 says, "Whoso putteth his trust in the Lord shall be safe." The world yearns for safety and security. Scripture says here that only the Lord can provide it.

   Proverbs 28:25 says, "He who trusts in the Lord will prosper" (NASB). That doesn't mean we will be always healthy, wealthy, and wise—as many preachers would have us believe today. It means as a person trusts in the Lord, the Lord will guide His steps, wherever that may lead. Note that the apostle Paul says in 1 Timothy 4:10: "We both labor and suffer reproach, because we trust in the living God." Based on this verse, could you really trust God? There's a risk involved. Could you place your life in the hands of God and be secure that He would provide for you?

3. David trusted the Lord

   Perhaps no statement of this counsel is more beautiful than King David when he said, "Trust in the Lord, and do good; so shalt thou dwell in the land, and verily thou shalt be fed. Delight thyself also in the Lord, and he shall give thee the desires of thine heart. Commit thy way unto the Lord; trust also in him, and he shall bring it to pass" (Ps. 37:3-5). The Bible says that you can trust God. Only in Him is there no credibility gap.

4. Abraham trusted the Lord

   Abraham is the best example of a man who trusted God, especially for those in the Jewish community, as in Hebrews 6:13-20. He is the most outstanding example of faith in the Old Testament and is called "the father of all them that believe" (Rom. 4:11, cf. Gal. 3:7).

   The writer is saying to the unbelieving Hebrews, "If it's not enough for you to look at the faithful in your own community (vv. 9-12), look at the example of a man from your own history and see how he trusted God." The writer knew they were beset by persecution from their own Jewish community, so he gave them an illustration from their own race of one who trusted God for everything in the midst of unbelievable adversity. He wanted to show them a man who went to the point of lifting a knife to slay his only son. Abraham was prepared to kill every hope that God had given him (cf. Gen. 22:1-18).

That is how much he trusted in God. Abraham then becomes the theme of Hebrews 6:13-20.

a) The courage of Abraham

(1) Romans 4—Paul said, "What saith the scripture? Abraham believed God, and it was counted unto him for righteousness. Now to him that worketh is the reward not reckoned of grace, but of debt. But to him that worketh not, but believeth on him that justifieth the ungodly, his faith is counted for righteousness" (vv. 3-5).

(a) His faith

The thrust of Romans 4 is that Abraham was saved—justified, counted righteous by God —because of his faith. And he not only was saved by faith before the Old (Mosaic) Covenant was given, but he also was saved even before he was circumcised, which was the mark of the covenant God made with Abraham (vv. 9-10). Paul's point is that salvation has never been by obedience to the law or by the performance of any rite but has always been by faith.

Whenever the New Testament writers spoke to a Jewish audience, they would invariably use Abraham as the basis of faith. They did so because the Jewish mind often assumed that salvation was gained by keeping the law, so Abraham was a way of showing that salvation comes by no other means than by faith.

(b) His race

Abraham was of the Jewish race in the sense that it began with him. He himself wasn't born into it. In fact, he was seventy-five years old and was not circumcised. The Jewish person often based his salvation on the fact that he was of Jewish descent and circumcised on the eighth day (cf. Phil. 3:4-6). But Abraham wasn't. He was righteous because he believed God. Verse 13 sums it up by saying, "For the promise that he should be the heir of the world was not to Abraham, or to his seed, through the law, but through the righteousness of faith."

(c) His age

God told Abraham that at ninety years of age, his wife, Sarah, was going to have a son. According to verses 20-22: "He staggered not at the promise of God through unbelief, but was strong in faith, giving glory to God, and being fully persuaded that, what he had promised, he was able to perform. And therefore it was imputed to him for righteousness."

(2) James 2:23—James carried the same idea when he said, "The scripture was fulfilled which saith, Abraham believed God, and it was imputed unto him for righteousness; and he was called the friend of God." Righteousness for Abraham came from believing God. Salvation, even in the Old Testament, was not by law but by faith.

b) The character of Abraham

What sort of faith did Abraham have? Why was it so significant, so exemplary, that he would be called the father of the faithful? Because Abraham believed God as far as one could humanly believe.

(1) He turned from false gods

Abraham, whose original name was Abram, was raised a pagan. He was a descendant of Shem, one of Noah's three sons. But apparently for many generations, his family had worshiped false gods. He grew up in Ur, an ancient Chaldean city of Mesopotamia.

(2) He obeyed God's commands

(a) He was willing to go to Canaan

God spoke to Abram and commanded him to go to Canaan. Hebrews 11:8 says, "By faith Abraham, when he was called to go out into a place which he should after receive for an inheritance, obeyed; and he went out, not knowing where he went." With no guarantee but God's Word that he would get there, Abraham believed God and went. The Lord promised Abraham that He would give Canaan to him and his descendants and that through Abraham all the families of the earth would be blessed (Gen. 12:1-3). The reiteration of that promise to Abraham is also found in Genesis 13:15-17; 15:5-6; 17:1-8; 18:18; and 22:18.

(b) He was willing to sacrifice Isaac

After Isaac, the promised son, was finally born and had become a teenager, God commanded Abraham to sacrifice him. Having no idea of the Lord's reasons or what would happen, Abraham obeyed. He obeyed because he believed God. Had not God miraculously intervened and provided a substitute sacrifice, Abraham would have slain Isaac on Mount Moriah. Yet Abraham's faith was not blind. He could not see the consequences of his obedience, but he could see God's character. Abraham had a gilt-edged security. When the Lord makes a promise, He puts his integrity on the line. Every promise of God is secured by His character.

Although Abraham is highlighted in Hebrews 6:13-20, the overriding theme behind these verses is the person and character of God. Can we trust our lives to God? Can we take Him at His word? Can He keep us from falling? Can He finish the work He has begun in us? Will He lose hold of us at some point along the line? In short, is there really salvation and security with God? Abraham believed there was. The Bible says there is. Hebrews 6:13-20 gives four unchanging guarantees on why we can trust God: His person, His purpose, His pledge, and His priest.

Lesson

I. GOD'S PERSON (vv. 13-15)

"When God made promise to Abraham, because he could swear by no greater, he swore by himself, saying, Surely, blessing I will bless thee, and multiplying I will multiply thee. And so, after he had patiently endured, he obtained the promise."

A. He Cannot Lie (v. 13)

No one in the universe is greater than God. Because God is who He is, He cannot lie. And the reason God cannot lie is that He invented truth. By definition of His very nature, whatever God says is absolute truth. It is absolutely impossible for God to lie (v. 18). He has no ability to contradict Himself. His promises, then, are secured by His person. That is why God's promise to Abraham (v. 13) was as good as done (v. 15).

1. His Word

God is the source of truth. Whatever He does is right and whatever He says is truth. Jesus said in His high priestly prayer, "Sanctify them through thy truth; thy word is truth" (John 17:17). Every word that comes out of the mouth of God is absolute truth.

2. His promise

If God makes a promise, He will keep it. Second Peter 3:9 says, "The Lord is not slack concerning his promise." The word *slack* means that there is no gap between God's promise and the fulfillment. As He says it, it happens. It is true because of His nature. The writer of Hebrews was telling his unsaved Jewish readers that they could trust God concerning the Messiah because He cannot lie.

In his opening statement to Titus, Paul says, "In hope of eternal life, which God, who cannot lie, promised before the world began" (1:2). Long ago God promised eternal life for those who come to Him, and He cannot lie.

3. His gift

James 1:17 says, "Every good gift and every perfect gift is from above, and cometh down from the Father of lights, with whom is no variableness, neither shadow of turning." He never deviates from His will or His promises. And throughout the New Testament, God promises again and again that if men come to Jesus Christ, they will have salvation, because He cannot lie. The apostle John said, "As many as received him, to them gave he power to become the children of God, even to them that believe on his name" (John 1:12).

B. He Cannot Lose (vv. 14-15)

Just as surely as God kept His promise to Abraham, He will keep His promise to those who trust in His Son. His basic promise to Abraham was, "Surely, blessing I will bless thee, and multiplying I will multiply thee" (v. 14). And that's what happened (v. 15). God was saying to Abraham, "I'm going to bless you and multiply your descendants." Did God keep His promise to Abraham? Indeed. Today there are several million physical descendants of Abraham. Not only that, but many more millions around the world are his spiritual descendants.

1. Abraham's doubt

God has never failed, and He never will. He told Abraham, "Look now toward heaven, and count the stars, if thou be able to number them: and he said unto him, So shall thy seed be" (Gen. 15:5). Abraham tried to help God along when he fathered a son, Ishmael, with Sarah's maid Hagar, but God used that as a punishment. Ishmael fathered the Arab race, which has been quarreling with the Jewish race ever since (cf. Gen. 16:12).

2. Abraham's devotion

Ultimately, though, Abraham believed God and was faithful to His promise. The writer of Hebrews says, "After he had patiently endured, he obtained the promise" (v. 15). As Abraham was continuing to be a faithful servant for God, God continued to give him the assurance of His divine plan. It must have looked like a complete impossibility in light of Sarah's age, but as Abraham trusted God, he saw God fulfill His promise. After Isaac was born, it must have been unthinkable for Abraham to be commanded to use him as a sacrifice. If Isaac died, it would appear that God had failed to keep His promise. Yet Abraham did not question God at all. He took Isaac to Mount Moriah and raised his hand to slay his only son, but God stayed his hand (Gen. 22:1-14). Abraham went that far because that's how much he believed God.

The stunning illustration of Abraham and Isaac can give us the confidence to trust God as well, even in the midst of severe trials. As Abraham and Isaac were walking up the mountain to worship, he assured his son that God would provide an acceptable sacrifice. We also can trust God as we're walking into seemingly insurmountable obstacles. God has asked us to present our bodies as a "living sacrifice, holy, acceptable unto God, which is your reasonable service" (Rom. 12:1). When Abraham was about to sacrifice his son, his eye landed on the ram in the thicket that God had already provided as the acceptable sacrifice. So, too, God has provided a sacrifice for us in the person of the Lord Jesus Christ. His thicket was a crown of thorns on His head (Matt. 27:29). God has never backed out of His promises nor will He. You can trust that God will never fail you. He has no capacity for failure because of who He is. Deuteronomy 31:8 says, "The Lord, he it is who doth go before thee; he will be with thee, he will not fail thee, neither forsake thee; fear not, neither be dismayed."

II. GOD'S PURPOSE (v. 14)

"[God was] saying, Surely, blessing I will bless thee, and multiplying I will multiply thee."

Abraham was secure not only because of God's Person but also because of God's purpose. God did not move Abraham from his homeland and make him a promise on some divine whim. God had a purpose for Abraham and for the world through him. It was not Abraham's idea but God's. His call of Abraham was entirely of His own doing.

A. God's Unfolding Plan for the World

The Abrahamic covenant—the promise from God to Abraham—was an unconditional covenant. God did not tell Abraham that he would be blessed if he met certain conditions. He *did* command things of Abraham and Abraham was obedient. But God's blessing was apart from Abraham; he was but a mere spectator—watching what God was doing for him and through him. God had a predetermined plan and purpose and He also determined that Abraham was the key man in that purpose.

1. After the Fall of man

   Not long after God created Adam and Eve and put them in His beautiful garden, where every one of their needs were met, they decided to do the one thing He had told them not to do. They ate from the tree of the knowledge of good and evil and fell, as did the rest of creation with them. As a result, the whole earth was cursed. Our first parents lost their fellowship with God and were exiled from Eden. Soon after that, the first murder was committed, and things went downhill from there (Gen. 4).

2. After the Flood on the earth

   Corruption, violence, polygamy, incest, lying, stealing,

adultery, idolatry, and every other kind of sin became common and increasingly worse. Mankind became so terribly debauched that God destroyed all people, except for the eight in Noah's family. In the generations after the Flood, man continued to depart from the Lord even though God tried to reach people through mediating His rule—first through Noah, who preached while he was building the ark, but no one would listen or change. Men were not responding to God's rule, and it became evident that God had to react in His wrath again.

3. After the fall of the Tower

The sinfulness of man reached a climax when, with the Tower of Babel, men literally tried to take heaven by storm (Gen. 11:1-9). God thwarted their scheme by causing them to speak different languages and then scattering them across the world.

B. God's Unconditional Promise to Abraham

But God did not give up on man. It was in His eternal plan that those whom He had created in His own image would worship and serve Him. It was as if there was once a flowing river that had been hit with a great landslide that now blocked it. But God began to cut a fresh channel. He picked out a certain people and used them as His channel of blessing against the landslide of sin that had inundated the world.

1. The channel

The first new channel for God's redemptive plan was Abraham, the father of the chosen people. From Abraham's loins was to come the nation of Israel, which would bring the salvation of the world through the Jewish Messiah. That is why Jesus said, "Salvation is of the Jews" (John 4:22). He did not mean that the Jews were the only ones who could be saved but that they were the channel through which salvation is secured.

2. The choosing

God predetermined the life of Abraham apart from Abraham choosing God. Abraham was only a spectator to the plan of God. It was a matter of divine choice. Abraham was saved because of his faith, but he wasn't chosen because of his faith. It was purely out of the sovereign will of God. Deuteronomy 7:7-8 says of Israel in general, "The Lord did not set His love on you nor choose you because you were more in number than any of the peoples, for you were the fewest of all the peoples, but because the Lord loved you and kept the oath which He swore to your forefathers" (NASB).

Many have been confused about how God chose Abraham apart from his faith. They say it seems as though God is simply using us as puppets in His plan. Genesis 18:18-19 helps to explain this concept. It says, "Seeing that Abraham shall surely become a great and mighty nation, and all the nations of the earth shall be blessed in him? For I know him." The phrase "for I know him" means that God had predetermined to love and choose Abraham. He set His love upon Abraham to be the one through whom the channel would be cut. Abraham was not chosen because of any merit, quality, or virtue. The phrase does not mean that God looked down for a faithful man—Abraham—and then subsequently chose him because of his faithfulness. That would make man sovereign, not God. But Abraham was chosen purely out of the sovereign will of God and not vice versa.

3. The covenant

When the Lord made the actual covenant with Abraham, He did it again apart from Abraham's ability to keep his part of the covenant. God tells Abraham in Genesis 15:9-18: "Take me an heifer of three years old, and a she-goat of three years old, and a ram of three years old, and a turtledove, and a young pigeon. And he took unto him all these, and divided them in the midst, and laid each piece one against another: but the birds divided he not. And when the fowls came down upon the carcasses, Abram drove them away. And when the sun was going down, a deep sleep fell upon Abram; and, lo, an horror of great darkness fell upon him. And he said unto Abram, Know of a surety that thy seed shall be a sojourner in a land that is not theirs, and shall serve them; and they shall afflict them four hundred years; and also that nation, whom they shall serve, will I judge: and afterward shall they come out with great substance. And thou shalt go to thy fathers in peace; thou shalt be buried in a good old age. But in the fourth generation they shall come here again; for the iniquity of the Amorites is not yet full. And it came to pass that, when the sun went down, and it was dark, behold a smoking furnace, and a burning lamp that passed between those pieces. In the same day the Lord made a covenant with Abram, saying, Unto thy seed have I given this land, from the river of Egypt unto the great river, the river Euphrates."

God made Abraham cut some specified animals in half and set the halves opposite each other. After God caused Abraham to fall into a deep sleep, the Lord spoke to him about his promise and then, in the form of a smoking oven and a flaming torch, passed between the halves Himself. Ordinarily, when such a covenant was made, both parties would walk between the pieces to symbolize their mutual obligations to fulfill the conditions agreed upon. But Abraham had no part in determining the conditions of this covenant or in the ceremony that sealed it. The fact that only God walked between the pieces signified that the total responsibility for fulfilling the covenant was His. Abraham was not a party to the covenant; only a recipient of it and a vehicle for its fulfillment. The covenant was made with Abraham in the sense that, humanly speaking, it revolved around him. But the conditions and obligations were God's alone. The covenant was made between God and Himself.

C. God's Unfolding Purpose for Israel

The nation of Israel was supposed to be a channel of blessing, but in what way? What were they supposed to do—for Him and by Him—in helping fulfill His purpose of redeeming a lost world? To cut through the landslide of sin that blocked the human stream, the channel of Israel was given seven purposes.

1. To proclaim the true God

Their job in the midst of idolatry, polytheism, polydemonism, and animism was to proclaim the true God. Their duty was summarized in Isaiah 43:21: "This people have I formed for myself; they will show forth my praise." They were not to be involved with any other god for Scripture says, "The Lord our God is one Lord" (Deut. 6:4).

2. To reveal the Messiah

The Jewish people were designed by God to reveal the Anointed One, who would be the great Savior of the world. Jesus was to be of Judaistic heritage. Just as surely as the prophets and psalmists were to proclaim His coming, so was the whole nation (cf. Ps. 110; Isa. 42; 53; Zech. 6:12-13).

3. To be a nation of priests

As the Mosaic covenant was being given to Israel at Mount Sinai, Israel was told by God, "If ye will obey my voice indeed, and keep my covenant, then ye shall be a peculiar treasure unto me above all people; for all the earth is mine: and ye shall be unto me a kingdom of priests, and an holy nation. These are the words which thou shalt speak unto the children of Israel" (Ex. 19:5-6). The nation of Israel was to represent God to the world. They were designed by Him to dispense His truth.

4. To preserve and transmit Scripture

Israel was also to be God's agents in depositing His Word to the world. In Deuteronomy 6:6-9 God instructs them by saying, "These words, which I command thee this day, shall be in thine heart; and thou shalt teach them diligently unto thy children, and shalt talk of them when thou sittest in thine house, and when thou walkest by the way, and when thou liest down, and when thou risest up. And thou shalt bind them for a sign upon thine hand, and they shall be as frontlets between thine eyes. And thou shalt write them upon the posts of thy house, and on thy gates." The Israelites were the transmitters of Scripture. All of the Old Testament and practically all of the New was written by Jewish people (cf. Rom. 9:4).

5. To show the faithfulness of God

The Israelites were also designed to be a living illustration of God's faithfulness to His people. Over and over again they failed God, but He always showed His faithfulness to them. Anyone who wanted to find out if God was faithful needed only to look at Israel. Even if Israel had always been faithful, their faithfulness could never have matched His. God is still not through in His dealings with Israel. The apostle Paul said that in the future, "All Israel shall be saved" (Rom. 11:26). The reason is given in verse 29: "The gifts and calling of God are without repentance." Those who say God has forsaken Israel and from now on deals only in the church malign God's Word and His faithfulness. Israel has been, still is, and will yet be a living illustration of His faithfulness.

6. To show the blessedness of serving God

The psalmist said, "Happy is that people . . . whose God is the Lord" (Ps. 144:15). The Israelites not only were to be a channel of His blessing but also an illustration of it.

7. To show God's grace in dealing with sin

The sacrificial system was God's gracious provision for dealing with sin. Although the sacrifices could not in themselves remove sin, they were a beautiful portrayal of how God Himself would remove it—through the blood of the perfect sacrifice of His own Son, Jesus Christ (cf. Heb. 9:11-14).

D. God's Unalterable Program for Mankind

God's purpose for Israel was to reveal His word to mankind. And God will never change His purposes because they are unalterable. Abraham was just as secure as the eternal plan of God. Jeremiah said, "Every purpose of the Lord shall be performed" (Jer. 51:29). God designed a channel—Israel—that through it, the world would be blessed. Isaiah said, "The Lord of hosts hath sworn, saying, Surely as I have thought, so shall it come to pass; and as I have purposed, so shall it stand" (Isa. 14:24).

1. The security of Israel

The promise to Abraham and the promise to everyone who trusts in Christ are as secure as God Himself. The Psalmist says, "The counsel of the Lord stands forever" (Ps. 33:11, NASB). As a Christian, you are as secure as Abraham because God purposed before the world began to conform you to the image of Jesus Christ. If He erred on that promise, He would have broken His eternal purpose for the nation of Israel. Romans 9:8 shows the security of the promise that God gave to Abraham: "They who are the children of the flesh, these are not the children of God, but the children of the promise are counted as the seed." Paul was saying that it is not just the Jewish people who are God's chosen people but also those to whom God has given a promise.

Romans 9:11 says, "The children [Esau and Jacob] being not yet born, neither having done any good or evil, that the purpose of God according to election might stand, not of works, but of him that calleth" (v. 11). Of the two sons of Isaac, God chose Jacob. He did not choose them because they were good or evil. He chose them because it was His purpose to elect them. God had purposed to work through Jacob. Jacob was secure in the purpose of God before he was ever born. The obvious argument to this choosing is, "What shall we say then? Is there unrighteousness with God" (v. 14)? Paul's answer in verse 14 is, "God forbid." God is not unjust. He says, "I will have mercy on whom I will have mercy, and I will have compassion on whom I will have compassion" (v. 15). It all depends on God's purpose. Someone might respond then, "Why doth he yet find fault? For who hath resisted his will" (v. 19)? Paul is saying, "How could God blame me if I am a sinner? How could he find fault with me if I resist His will?" Paul again answers, "Who art thou that resist against God? Shall the thing formed say to him that formed it, why hast thou made me thus?" (v. 20).

Nothing is said about man's part—his work, faithfulness, or obedience. This passage explains the sovereign side of God's plan and is alone the basis of man's security. God has purposed to love His own and nothing can violate that plan. When God designs His purposes, He carries them out. God's plan for Israel might have been set aside for a time, but He will again regather His people because His plans never fail (cf. Rom. 11:26).

2. The security of the believer

    God has secured a place in His future plans not only for Israel but also for everyone who embraces the Lord Jesus Christ. God's plan for the believer is to conform him to the image of His Son.

    a) Ephesians 1:3-5—Paul said, "Blessed be the God and Father of our Lord Jesus Christ, who hath blessed us with all spiritual blessings in heavenly places in Christ, according as he hath chosen us in him before the foundation of the world, that we should be holy and without blame before him, in love having pre-destinated us unto the adoption of sons by Jesus Christ to himself, according to the good pleasure of his will." Nothing is said at all in those verses to indicate that the believer has done anything to secure his own salvation. God, according to His own purpose, is the One who secures salvation for the believer. And if man cannot secure his own salvation, he also cannot keep his own salvation. God will both save the believer and keep the believer saved.

b) Romans 8:28-30—Paul said, "We know that all things work together for good to them that love God, to them who are the called according to his purpose. For whom he did foreknow, he also did predestinate to be conformed to the image of his Son, that he might be the first-born among many brethren. Moreover, whom he did predestinate, them he also called; and whom he called, them he also justified; and whom he justified, them he also glorified." The promise is so certain that Paul puts it in the past tense—even for future believers. Everyone that God foreordained, He also predestined to be conformed to Jesus Christ. That means everyone who comes to salvation will be conformed to Jesus Christ. No one is lost in the middle. Paul goes on in the rest of the chapter to explain that there is no other authority that can dispute God's claim on the believer. That is why Jesus could say at the end of His earthly ministry, "While I was with them in the world, I kept them in my name; those that thou gavest me I have kept, and none of them is lost" (John 17:12).

III. GOD'S PLEDGE (vv. 13b, 16-18)

"Because he could swear by no greater, he swore by himself. . . . For men verily swear by the greater, and an oath for confirmation is to them an end of all strife. Wherein God, willing more abundantly to show unto the heirs of promise the immutability of his counsel, confirmed it by an oath, that by two immutable things, in which it was impossible for God to lie, we might have a strong consolation, who have fled for refuge to lay hold upon the hope set before us."

A. Man's Custom (v. 16)

It was common in New Testament times for a person to make an oath on something or someone greater than himself. That is the meaning of verse 16. Men would usually swear by the altar, the high priest, or even God. Once such an oath was made, the argument was over. It would be assumed that if someone made such an oath, he was fully determined to keep it.

B. God's Concession (v. 17)

God, of course, does not need to make such an oath. His Word is every bit as good without an oath—as ours ought to be (cf. Matt. 5:33-37). But to accommodate the weak faith of men, God swore His promise to Abraham on Himself: "God, willing more abundantly to show unto the heirs of promise the immutability of his counsel, confirmed it by an oath" (v. 17). Since there is nothing greater than God, He swore by Himself (v. 13). That pledge did not make God's promise any more secure. He gave it nonetheless as further assurance to those who are slow to believe. The bare Word of God is guarantee enough, but God gave an oath just to show that He meant what He said.

1. The pledge of the Holy Spirit

   The pledge of God's oath to the believer is the presence of the Holy Spirit. Three times Paul referred to the Holy Spirit as God's pledge to believers (2 Cor. 1:22; 5:5). Ephesians 1:14 talks about the "earnest [Gk., *arrabōn*, "pledge"] of our inheritance." In modern Greek, *arrabōn* is used to refer to an engagement ring—a pledge of marriage. Because of God's gracious pledge, my salvation is secured by the Holy Spirit.

2. The promise of the Holy Spirit

   The writer of Hebrews also speaks about the recipients of God's promises. He says, "God, willing more abundantly to show unto the heirs of promise the immutability of his counsel, confirmed it by an oath" (v. 17). God did not simply give His promise to Abraham but to all spiritual heirs of the promise—all those who have put their faith in God throughout the ages. God's oath to Abraham stands as a testimony of God's faithfulness for all time. God's oath was given not only so that Abraham might be fully persuaded but so that all the heirs of Abraham's promise throughout the ages might know that God keeps His Word.

C. God's Character (v. 18)

The writer goes on to say, "By two immutable [Gk., *ametathetōn*] things, in which it was impossible for God to lie, we might have a strong consolation, who have fled for refuge to lay hold upon the hope set before us" (v. 18). The two immutable or unchangeable things spoken of here refer to God's promise and His pledge. *Ametathēton* was used in relation to wills. Once properly made, a will was unchangeable by anyone but the maker. God has declared His promise and His pledge to be unchangeable, even by Himself. His will cannot be switched, transposed, or altered.

1. The encouragement He gives

    The writer goes on to say, "It was impossible for God to lie" and "we might have a strong consolation." The phrase "strong consolation" comes from the Greek word *parakleō*, which means a "strong encouragement" or "strong confidence." The writer adds, "Who have fled for refuge." In the Septuagint, the Greek word for "refuge" is used for the cities God provided for those who sought protection from avengers for an accidental killing (cf. Num. 35; Deut. 19; Josh. 20). We will never know whether God can hold on to us until in desperation we run to Him for refuge.

2. The hope He gives

    The writer ends verse 18 by saying, "To lay hold upon the hope set before us." What is the hope that is set before us? Jesus Himself and the gospel He brought.

    a) 1 Timothy 1:1—Paul said, "The Lord Jesus Christ . . . is our hope."

    b) Colossians 1:5—Paul also said, "The hope which is laid up for you in heaven, of which ye heard before in the word of the truth of the gospel." If you are ever going to have a strong confidence and a steadfast hope, you must flee to God as a refuge and embrace Jesus Christ, who is your only hope of salvation.

IV. GOD'S PRIEST (vv. 19-20)

"Which hope we have as an anchor of the soul, both sure and steadfast, and which entereth into that within the veil, where the forerunner is for us entered, even Jesus, made an high priest forever after the order of Melchizedek."

A. The Anchor (v. 19)

In the New Covenant God added yet another security: Jesus Christ. As our High Priest, Jesus serves as the anchor of our souls, the One who will forever keep us from drifting away from God. The believer is anchored to God by His relationship with Christ and can be confident because it is "within the veil" (v. 19). In the Old Testament, the most sacred place in the Temple was the Holy of Holies, which is where the sacrifice of atonement was made. Inside the Holy of Holies was the Ark of the Covenant, which signified the glory of God. Only once a year on the day of atonement, the high priest would make atonement for the sins of the children of Israel. But under the New Covenant, atonement has been made once for all time by Christ's sacrifice on the cross. Our soul is, in God's mind, already secured within the veil—His eternal sanctuary.

B. The Assurance (v. 20)

When Jesus entered the heavenly Holy of Holies, He did not leave, as did the Aaronic high priests. Rather, "He . . . sat down on the right hand of the Majesty on high" (Heb. 1:3). And Jesus remains there forever as the Guardian of our souls. Such absolute security is almost incomprehensible. Not only are our souls anchored within the impregnable, inviolable heavenly sanctuary, but our Savior, the Lord Jesus Christ, stands guard over them as well. How can the Christian's security be described as anything but eternal? Truly we can trust God and His Savior with our souls. That is good cause to get off the fence and come all the way to salvation.

Focusing on the Facts

1. Why is there such a distrust of people in the world (see pp. 66-67)?
2. _____ in the _____ with all your heart is the only real answer in today's _____ world (see p. 67).
3. Who is the father of faith? Support your answer with Scripture (see p. 68).
4. What was the writer of Hebrews urging the Jewish community to do (see p. 68)?
5. What is the theme of Hebrews 6:13-20 (see p. 69)?
6. True or False: Abraham is a wonderful example of faith because he trusted God against all odds (see p. 69).
7. Why do the New Testament writers often use Abraham as the basis of faith (see p. 69)?
8. Abraham was not circumcised before God called him to lead the Jewish race. Why is that so important (see p. 69)?
9. True or False: Salvation in the Old Testament was by keeping the law of God (see pp. 69-70).
10. What is the overriding security in Hebrews 6:13-20 (see p. 71)?
11. Did God keep His promise to Abraham? Explain (see p. 72).

12. What kind of illustration can Abraham and Isaac provide for someone today (see p. 73)?

13. What were the three main problems that arose in the unfolding plan of God? How did God deal with those situations (see pp. 74-75)?

14. What was Abraham's role in the plan of God? Did Abraham have to remain absolutely obedient if God's plan was to succeed (see pp. 75-76)?

15. What was different about God's covenant with Abraham (see pp. 76-77)?

16. What were some of the ways in which Israel was to be God's channel of blessing to the rest of the world (see pp. 77-79)?

17. What was the apostle Paul's response to those who said man has no say in God's choosing process (Rom. 9:20; see p. 79)?

18. God's plan for the believer is to conform him to the image of _____ (see p. 80).

19. What is meant by the pledge of the Spirit (see p. 82)?

20. What is the hope that is set before us, and why is it important (Heb. 6:18; see pp. 83-84)?

21. What is the significance of the priesthood as discussed in verses 19-20 (see p. 83)?

22. Discuss the Old Testament form for atonement and explain Christ's death on the cross in the New Testament in relation to it (see p. 84).

Pondering the Principles

1. The theme of Hebrews 6:13-20 is the security of God's promises. Several things stand out in the passage but most important are Abraham's faith and God's faithfulness. Do you believe that God will supply all you need to live the Christian life? Read the following verses, and ask God to strengthen your faith in Him: Numbers 23:19, 2 Timothy 2:13, Titus 1:2, and Hebrews 6:18.

2. Israel was designed by God to be His channel of blessing to the world in seven ways (see pp. 77-79). It could also be said in a secondary sense that the church has the same responsibilities. Match the following passages from the New Testament to the purposes that follow:

a) Proclaiming God   a) Ephesians 1:3
b) Revealing the Messiah b) Ephesians 2:8-9
c) Being a nation of priests c) 1 Thessalonians 5:24
d) Preserving Scripture   d) Jude 3
e) Showing God's faithfulness e) Acts 2:36
f) Showing God's blessing f) 1 Peter 2:9
g) Showing God's grace   g) John 1:1, 14

Scripture Index